The Science of BECOMING EXCELLENT

Wallace D. Wattles
and
Dr. Judith Powell

TOP OF THE MOUNTAIN PUBLISHING
Largo, Florida 34643-5117 U.S.A.

TOP OF THE MOUNTAIN PUBLISHING
A Division of Powell Productions
P.O. Box 2244, Pinellas Park, Florida 33780-2244
U.S.A.
SAN 287-590X
CATALOG ONLINE: http://www.AbcInfo.Com
E-MAIL: rich@abcinfo.com
PHONE (727) 391-3958 * FAX (727) 391-4598

1st printing 1993 - 2nd printing 1997
3rd printing 2000 - 4rd printing 2002

Library of Congress Cataloging Publication Data
Wattles, Wallace Delois
The science of becoming excellent / by Wallace D. Wattles and Judith L. Powell.
p. cm.
Includes bibliographical references.
ISBN 0-914295-96-9, quality pbk.: $8.95
1.Self-actualization (Psychology).
I. Powell, Judith L. II. Title.
BF637.S4W39 1993 158'1-dc20 92-41455 CIP

Cover Design: Dr. Tag Powell
Manufactured in the United States of America

CONTENTS

FOREWORD

There is a special influence in all of nature which carries us in the direction of final fulfillment. What is this special influence? It is all-pervading and forever-available. It is life's natural inclination towards the direction of unfoldment, growth, and completion. To harmonize with this influence is to experience certain success in all useful ventures.

We are a combination of spiritual qualities and material elements. The eternal aspect of us is divine and is, therefore, immortal. Because of our essential divine nature, we are designed to prosper – to thrive, to flourish, and to be successful. If we are not thriving, if we are not flourishing, if we are not being successful, we have lessons yet to learn. *Learning our lessons and actualizing our innate soul qualities is the very purpose of human existence.* We might as well do all we can to fulfill the purpose for our being here in this world.

You are designed to experience total completion. You are designed to be spiritually aware, mentally creative, emotionally well, physically vital, happy in relationships, and to be a goal-

Learning our lessons and actualizing our innate soul qualities is the very purpose of human existence.

achiever. To settle for only partial fulfillment is error, and you will never be truly satisfied until you rise above and are free of all barriers which restrict and limit the soul's aspirations.

I am pleased to be asked to write this brief foreword to this tremendous book. It has been a classic for decades because it speaks to the heart and stirs the fires of the soul. The reader can only benefit from a careful study and application of these principles which are so well shared.

ROY EUGENE DAVIS

Roy Eugene Davis is director of Center For Spiritual Awareness which has world headquarters at Lakemont, Georgia. As an author of over twenty books and a world-traveled speaker on principles of mind and consciousness, he shares with many people the guidelines offered in the book you now hold in your hands. Mr. Davis may be contacted at Box 7, Lakemont, Georgia 30552.

INTRODUCTION

The average person's idea of a *great person*, rather than of one who serves, is of one who succeeds in getting themselves served. According to the average person, a great person attains positions to command others; to exercise power over them, making them obey. The exercise of dominion over other people, to most people, is a great thing. Nothing seems to be sweeter to the selfish soul than this. You will always find every selfish and undeveloped person trying to domineer over others, to exercise control over others.

Savage men were no sooner placed upon the earth than they began to enslave one another. For ages the struggle in war, diplomacy, politics, and government has been aimed at securing control over other people. Kings and Queens have drenched the soil of the earth in blood and tears in the effort to extend their dominions and their power – to rule more people.

The struggle of the business world today is the same as that on the battlefields of Europe half a century ago so far as the ruling principle is concerned. Why do individuals with a net worth of hundreds of millions, even billions, seek for more money and make themselves slaves to the business struggle when they already have more than they can possibly use? It is a kind of madness. "Suppose a man had fifty thousand pairs of pants, seventy-five thousand shirts, one hundred thousand coats, and one hundred and fifty thousand neckties, what would you think of him if he woke in the morning before daybreak and worked until after it was dark every day, rain or shine, in all kinds of weather, merely to get another necktie?"

But this is not a good simile. The possession of neckties gives a man no power over others, while the possession of dollars does. The top 10% of wealthy people are not after dollars but power! It is the principle of the Pharisee; while the Pharisees were just and righteous men, honorable judges, true lawgivers and upright in their dealings with people, they loved the uppermost seats at feasts and greeting in the market place, and to be called Master – it is the struggle for the high place. Power develops able individuals, cunning individuals, resourceful individuals, but not great individuals.

Contrast these two ideas of greatness sharply in your minds. "He who will be great among you let him serve." Stand before the average American audience and ask the name of the greatest American and the majority will think of Abraham Lincoln; and is this not because in Lincoln, above all the other people who has served us in public life, we recognize the spirit of service? Not servility, but service. Lincoln was a great man because he knew how to be a great servant. Napoleon, able, cold, selfish, seeking the high places, was a brilliant man. However, unlike Lincoln who was great, Napoleon was not. In today's world, H. Ross Perot talks about bringing the government leaders back to being servants of the people – to work FOR them (not against them).

The very moment you begin to advance and are recognized as one who is doing things in a Great Way you will find yourself in danger. The temptation to patronize, advise, or take upon yourself the direction of other people's affairs is sometimes almost irresistible. Help others to help themselves, not to become dependent upon you for their needs. Avoid, however, the opposite danger of falling into servility, or of completely throwing yourself away in the service of others. To do this has been the ideal of many people. The completely self-sacrificing life has been thought to be the Christ-like life because of the complete misconceptions of the character and teachings of religions.

Thousands of people imitating Jesus and other Masters, as they supposed, have belittled themselves and given up all else to go about doing good; practicing an altruism that is really as morbid and as far from great as the rankest selfishness. There are other things you must do besides helping the unfortunate, although it is true that a large part of the life and activities of every great person must be given to helping other people. As you begin to advance they will come to you. Do not turn them away. But do not make the fatal error of supposing that a life of complete self-denial is the way of greatness.

Practice all the steps outlined in this book... lift your mind and spirit to excellence and you will already be helping others by advancing the human race.

Very Truly yours
W. D. Wattles
DR. Judith Powell

CHAPTER ONE

AWAKENING TO EXCELLENCE

There is a *Principle of Power* in every person. By the intelligent use and direction of this principle you can achieve excellence; you can develop your own mental faculties. You have an inherent power by which you may grow in whatever direction you please, and there does not appear to be any limit to the possibilities of your growth.

...genius is the union of human and Creator in the acts of the soul.

No one has yet become so great in any faculty that it isn't possible for someone else to become greater. The possibility lies in the *Original Substance* from which we and all are made. *Genius is Omniscience flowing into us. Genius is more than talent* – talent may merely be one faculty developed out of proportion to other faculties – *but genius is the union of human and Creator in the acts of the soul.* Great individuals are always greater than their deeds. They are in connection with a reserve power that is without limit. We do not know where the location of the boundary of our mental power is; we do not even know that there is a boundary!

The power of *conscious* growth is not given to the lower animals; it is ours alone and may be developed and increased by us. The lower animals can, to a great extent, be trained and developed by us; but we can consciously train and develop ourselves. We alone have this power, and we have it to an apparently unlimited extent.

The purpose of life for you is growth, just as the purpose of life for trees and plants is growth. Trees and plants grow where they are planted automatically and along fixed lines; you can grow and move as you will. Trees and plants can only develop certain possibilities and characteristics; you can develop any power which is or has been shown by any person, anywhere, any time.

> ✷ *Nothing* that is possible in spirit is impossible in flesh and blood.
>
> ✷ *Nothing* that man can think is impossible in action.
>
> ✷ *Nothing* that man can imagine is impossible of realization.

Human beings are formed for growth and we are under the necessity of growing. *It is essential to our happiness that we should continuously advance.*

Life without progress becomes endurable – and the person who ceases to grow must either become imbecile, or insane, or "burned-out." To be burned-out is nothing more than to be bored with things as they are... to be bored is to stagnate... and to stagnate is not to advance as a human. The greater and more harmonious and well-rounded your growth, the happier you will be.

There is no possibility in any individual that is not in *us all.* But if all proceeds naturally, no two of us will grow into the same thing, nor be alike, even for identical twins. Everyone comes into the world with a *predisposition to grow along certain lines*, and growth is easier for them along those lines than in any other way. This is Nature's wise provision, for it gives *endless variety.* This is what we term *destiny.*

It is as if a gardener should throw all his bulbs into one basket. To the superficial observer they would look alike, but growth reveals a tremendous difference. So of men and women; they are like the basket of bulbs. One may be a rose and add brightness and color to some dark corner of the world... one may be a lily and teach a lesson of love and purity to every eye that sees... one may be a climbing vine and hide the rugged outlines of some dark rock... one may be a great oak among whose branches the birds will nest and sing. But each one will be something worthwhile, something rare, and something uniquely perfect.

There are undreamed of possibilities in the common lives all around us; in a large sense, there are no "common" people. In times of national stress and peril, the homeless people and the lowest alcoholic and addict become heroes and ambassadors through the quickening of the *Principle of Power* within them.

There is a genius quality in every man and woman, waiting to be brought forward.

There is a genius quality in every man and woman, and it is waiting to be brought forward. Every city has its great man or woman; someone to whom all go for advice in times of trouble; someone who is instinctively recognized as being great in wisdom and insight. To such a person the minds of the whole community turn in times of local crisis; that individual is silently recognized as being great. They do small things in an excellent way. They could do great things in an excellent way as well if they just undertake them; so can any one... so can you!

The *Principle of Power* gives us just what we ask of it—if we only undertake little things, it only gives us power for little things; but if we try to do great things in a Great Way, it gives us all the power there is. But beware of undertaking great things in a small way, which we will discuss later.

There are two *mental attitudes* an individual may take:

* ONE makes that person like a *football*. It has resilience and reacts strongly when force is applied to it, but it originates nothing. It never acts of its own accord; there is no power within it. People of this type are controlled by circumstance and environment; their destinies are decided by things external to themselves; the *Principle of Power* within them is never really active at all. They never speak or act from within.

* The SECOND attitude develops individuals into a *flowing spring*. Power comes out from the center of them; coming from within them like a well of water springing up into everlasting life. They radiate force; they are felt by their environment. The *Principle of Power* within them is in constant action; they are *self-active*.

No greater good can come to any man or woman than to become self-active. *All the experiences of life are designed by Providence to force men and women into self-activity*; to compel them to cease being creatures of circumstance and master their environment. All the seemingly positive and negative happenings in your life are opportunities given to *you* by Fate, for *you* to take control; for *you* to design your own destiny!

All the experiences of life are designed by Providence to force men and women into self-activity... for you to take control; for you to design your own destiny.

SUMMARY

In our lowest stage, we are the children of chance and circumstance, and the slaves of fear. Your acts are all *reactions* resulting from the forces imposed on you in your environment. You act only as you are acted upon; you originate nothing. But even the lowest human has within them a *Principle of Power* sufficient to master all that they fear; and if they learn this and become self-active, they become as one of the gods – a truly *Thinking Being.*

The awakening of the Principle of Power in you is the real conversion; the passing from death to life.

It is the resurrection and the life. When excellence is awakened, you become one with the Highest and all power is given to you on earth and in heaven; in mind and in spirit.

Nothing was ever in any person that is not in you; no one ever had more spiritual or mental power than you can attain, or did greater things than you can accomplish. You can become what you want to be. *Awaken to excellence!*

CHAPTER TWO

BEYOND PREDISPOSITION

You are not barred from attaining excellence by heredity. No matter who or what your ancestors may have been or how unlearned or lowly their status, the upward way is open for you. There is no such thing as inheriting a fixed mental position; no matter how small the mental ability we receive from our parents, it may be increased. *No one is born incapable of growth.*

> *An inherited mental trait is a habit of thought that your father or mother impressed upon your inner-conscious mind.*

Heredity counts for something. We are born with some innerconscious mental tendencies. For instance, a tendency to depression, or fear, or to anger—but all these inner-conscious tendencies may be overcome. When the real you awakens and comes forward you can easily throw off any depleting tendencies. Nothing of this kind needs to keep you down. If you have inherited undesirable mental tendencies, you can eliminate them and put desirable tendencies in their places.

An inherited mental trait is a habit of thought that your father or mother impressed upon your inner-conscious mind. Now you can substitute the opposite impression by forming the opposite habit of thought. You can substitute a habit of cheerfulness for a tendency to depression; you *can* overcome fear or anger.

Heredity may count for something, too, in an inherited shape of the skull. There is something in phrenology (the study of the "bumps" and shape of the skull) if not so much as its exponents claim. It is true that the different faculties are localized in the brain, and that the power of a faculty depends upon the number of active brain cells in its area. A mental faculty whose brain area is large is likely to act with more power than one whose cranial section is small; so possibly, persons with certain conformations of the skull show talent as musicians, lecturers, mechanics, and so on.

It has been argued from this that a person's cranial formation must, to a great extent, decide their status in life, but this is an error. It has been found that a small brain section, with many fine and active cells, gives as powerful expression to faculty as a larger brain with coarser cells. And it has been found that *by focusing the Principle of Power on any section of the brain, with the will and purpose to develop a particular talent, the brain cells may be multiplied indefinitely.*

Any faculty, power, or talent you possess, no matter how small or embryonic, may be increased – you can multiply the brain cells in its particular area until it acts as powerfully as you wish. It is true that you can act most easily through those faculties that are now largely developed. You can do, with the least effort, the things which "come naturally"; but it is also true that if you will make the necessary effort, you can develop any talent.

The brain does not make the person; the person (thought and character) makes the brain. For you are not just a brain; you are the sum of brain, mind and spirit.

You can do what you desire to do, and become what you want to be. When you fix upon some ideal and proceed using the principles in this book, all the power of your being is focused on the faculties required in the realization of that ideal. More blood and nerve force go to the corresponding sections of the brain, and the cells are quickened, increased, and multiplied in number. The proper use of your mind will build a brain capable of doing what you direct your mind to do.

The brain does not make the person; the person (thought and character) makes the brain. For you are not just a brain; you are the sum of brain, mind and spirit. Your brain does not intelligently think on its own – it is an organ of the body just as is the heart. However, just as you can learn to control your heart rate using your mind – thought, you too can learn to quicken your brain cells. Mind influences the brain; and the brain influences the body; spirit oversees all. Draw upon the *Principle of Power* to help guide you from predisposition.

Your place in life is not fixed by *heredity*. Nor are you condemned to the lower levels by circumstances or by lack of opportunity. The *Principle of Power* within you is sufficient for all the requirements of your soul. No possible combination of circumstances can keep you down: If you adjust your personal attitude towards the right direction and determine to rise. The Power which formed you and programmed you for growth also controls the circumstances of society, industry, and government; and this Power is never divided against Itself. The Power which is in you is in the things around you, and when you begin to move forward, the things will arrange themselves for your advantage, as described in later chapters of this book.

✱ FACT: *Poverty is no barrier to excellence, for poverty can always be removed.* Linnaeus the naturalist, had only forty dollars with which to educate himself. He mended his own shoes and often had to beg meals from his friends. Michael Cane grew up in the cockney slums, in a family of generations of fish porters. They had no electricity in their home until he was 13 years old. Michael turned it all around and became one of our great actors of stage and film.

✸ FACT: *Wealth and breeding is no assurance to excellence.* There have been tens of thousands of men and women of noble birth, or who have been born in well-to-do families, but few have achieved greatness. Some of whom have achieved excellence are: Siddhartha Buddha, Queen Elizabeth I, Queen Victoria, Peter the Great, Catherine the Great, Eleanor Roosevelt, John F. Kennedy.

✸ FACT: *Race or background is no barrier to excellence.* Leontyne Price, born in Mississippi to a carpenter and midwife, grew up in the racially-torn South in the 1940's. She so impressed the townspeople, both white and black, that they funded her musical training. Leontyne was the first

Black-American to achieve international operatic superstardom, denied to her great predecessors, Marian Anderson and Paul Robson. Born *illegitimately* (which at that time was *supposed to be* a barrier), to a married woman and a ne'er-do-well son of a Scottish Lord, Alexander (Fawcett) Hamilton went on to achieve excellence as the first Secretary of the Treasury of the United States. He also founded the Bank of New York.

✱ *FACT: Lack of education is no bar to excellence, for living life to the fullest is in itself an education.* Wally Amos, the founder of Famous Amos Cookies, was poor and was illiterate. Not only has he achieved great business success, he is now extremely active in a humanitarian role—bringing excellent literacy programs to the populace by way of television. In fact, you will find that many geniuses, inventors, and great personalities never finished high school, with many never going past the sixth grade! They couldn't sit back on their *educated laurels*... they were motivated to activate their *grey cells* through Thought and Action. Some people with advanced education feel that the *world owes them* a living (presumably because they had to suffer the rigors of schooling), rather than *they owing the world* fruits from their expanded mind and spirit!

✸ *FACT: Lack of physical health is no bar to excellence.* Stephen Hawking, diagnosed as having Lou Gehrig's disease when in graduate school, went on to earn an international reputation as the most brilliant theoretical physicist since Einstein. From his viewpoint in a wheelchair, he has brought to light expanded theories of the nature of time and the universe. Franklin Delano Roosevelt, diagnosed with polio, served three terms in office during peacetime and during wartime, from a wheelchair. He went on to become one of the most beloved presidents of the United States. Scott Hamilton was a sickly child, and he went on to win a gold medal in men's figure skating at the 1984 Winter Olympics. Many athletes, in extreme physical pain while performing, have gone on to attain the prestigious Gold Medal.

✱ FACT: *Age and gender are no barriers to excellence.* Louis Pasteur, who discovered that heat kills germs (pasteurization) as well as developed immune vaccinations, made some of his greatest scientific discoveries after suffering a stroke when he was over 50 years old. Marie Curie was awarded two Nobel Prizes in science. Amelia Earhart, in a male-dominated profession, was the first woman to fly over the Atlantic alone.

Don't make the mistake of associating genius with just scientific or medical discoveries. There are many individuals, living at various times, from a myriad of backgrounds who have awakened their genius faculties toward excellence: Michelangelo, Da Vinci, Galileo, Newton, Thomas Jefferson, De Gaulle, Benjamin Franklin, Edison, Alexander

Graham Bell, Marconi, Nikola Tesla, Elisha Gray, Joseph Swan, Oprah Winfrey, Margaret Thatcher, Marcus Aurelius, Churchill, Jonas Salk, Mother Theresa, Dian Fossey, Jane Goodall, Margaret Mead, Walter Russell, Lee Iacocca, Henry Ford, Bill Cosby, Bach, Beethoven, General Norman Schwartzkopf, George Washington Carver, Mexican President Juarez, Quincy Jones, Joan of Arc, Olga Worrall, Edgar Cayce, Lao Tze, Mahatma Gandhi, Maharishi-Mahesh Yogi, Dale Carnegie, Jose Silva, Golda Meir, Ted Turner.

Discover greatness – read biographies and autobiographies of people of excellence.

SUMMARY

We were formed for growth, and all things external were designed to promote our growth. No sooner will you awaken your soul and enter on the Advancing Way then you find that not only is the Infinite for you, but nature, society, and your fellow humans, are also for you. Furthermore, all things work together for your good if you obey the law.

There is the *Principle of Power* in you; if you use it and apply it in a Certain Way you can overcome all heredity, master all circumstances and conditions, and become excellent and radiate a powerful personality.

CHAPTER THREE

THE SOURCE OF WISDOM

Your body, brain, mind, faculties, and talents are the mere instruments you use in demonstrating excellence – in themselves they do not make you great. A person may have a large brain and a good mind, strong faculties, and brilliant talents, and yet they are not a great person unless they *use* all these in a Great Way. That quality which enables you to use your abilities in a Great

Way makes you excellent; and to that quality we give the name of *wisdom.*

✸ 1. *Wisdom is the essential basis of greatness and excellence.*

✸ 2. *Wisdom is the power to perceive the best ends to aim at and the best means for reaching those ends. It is the power to perceive the right thing to do.* Anyone who is wise enough to know the right thing to do, who is good enough to wish to do only the right thing, and who is able and strong enough to do the right thing, is truly great. They will instantly become marked as a personality of power in any community, and people will delight to do them honor.

✸ 3. *Wisdom is dependent upon knowledge.* Where there is complete ignorance – no knowledge of the right thing to do – there can be no wisdom. Your knowledge is comparatively limited and so your wisdom must be small... unless you can connect your mind with a knowledge greater than your own and draw from it, *by inspiration* (the wisdom that your own limitations deny you). This you can do — *tap into the Source;* this is what the men and women of true excellence have done.

Only God knows all truths; therefore, only God can have real wisdom or know the right thing to do at all times. Keep in mind that *we can receive wisdom from God.* For example: Abraham Lincoln, sixteenth President of the United States, had limited education, but he had the power to perceive truth. For Lincoln it is apparent that real wisdom consists in *1) knowing* the right thing to do at all times and under all circumstances; *2)* in having the *will* to do the right thing; *3)* and in having *talent and ability* enough to be competent and able to do the right thing.

Back in the days of the abolition agitation, and during the compromise period, when all other men were more or less confused as to what was right or as to what ought to be done, Lincoln was never uncertain. He saw through the superficial arguments of the pro-slavery movement. He also saw, the impracticability and fanaticism of the

Knowledge of truth is not often reached by the processes of reason – it is due to a spiritual insight.

abolitionists. He envisioned the right ends to aim at, and he purposed the best means for which to attain those ends. It was because people recognized that he perceived truth and knew the right thing to do that they made him president.

When Lincoln became president he was surrounded by a multitude of so-called able advisers, hardly any two of whom would agree. At times they were all opposed to his policies; at times almost the whole North was opposed to what he proposed to do during the American Civil War. But he saw the truth when others were misled by appearances; his judgment was seldom or never wrong. He was at once the ablest statesman and the best soldier of the period.

Where did he, a comparatively unlearned, poor man, get this wisdom? It was not due to some peculiar shape of his skull or to some fineness of texture of his brain. It was not due to some physical characteristic. It was not even a quality of mind due to superior reasoning power. *Knowledge of truth is not often reached by the processes of reason*

> *...there can be no truth until there is a mind to perceive it. Truth does not exist apart from mind.*

– *it is due to a spiritual insight.* He perceived truth, but where did he perceive it, and where did the perception come from?

We see something similar in George Washington, the first President of the United States, whose faith and courage, due to his perception of truth, held the colonies together during the long and often apparently hopeless struggle of the American Revolution. We see something of the same thing in the phenomenal genius of General Patton, who always knew, in military matters, the best means to adopt during World War II in Europe. We see that the greatness of Patton was in nature rather than in Patton, and we discover behind Washington and Lincoln something greater than either Washington or Lincoln.

We see the same thing in all great men and women. They perceive truth, but truth cannot be perceived until it exists; and there can be no truth until there is a mind to perceive it. *Truth does not exist apart from mind.* Washington, Lincoln and Patton were in touch and communication with a

Mind which knows all knowledge and contains all truth. So true of all who manifest wisdom.

Wisdom is Knowledge *internalized* and acted upon in a just and right way. *Wisdom is obtained by reading the mind of Supreme Intelligence.*

SUMMARY

Anyone who develops the power to perceive truth, and who can show that they always know the right thing to do, and that they can be trusted to do the right thing, will be honored and advanced. The whole world is looking eagerly for such people. Become that type of person!

Attune your mind with All-Mind... act in a Certain Way and think in a Great Way. Link with Mind and you will see, feel, touch, and sense real Wisdom, not fiction. The simple truth will surround you on all sides on the outer level, on the inner level you will think truth; think as a part of Mind; think as a God.

CHAPTER FOUR

THE MIND OF THE SUPREME

There is a Cosmic Intelligence which is in all things and through all things. This is the one real substance; from it all things proceed. It is *Intelligent Substance* or *Mind Stuff.* It is God. Where there is no substance there can be no intelligence, for where there is no substance there is nothing.

Where there is thought there must be a substance which thinks.

✷ *FACT*: Thought cannot be function, for function is motion, and it is inconceivable that mere motion should think.

✷ *FACT*: Thought cannot be vibration, for vibration is motion, and that motion should be intelligent is not thinkable.

Motion is nothing but the moving of substance. If there is intelligence shown it must be in the substance and not in the motion. Thought cannot be the result of motions in the brain. If thought is in the brain it must be in the brain's substance and not in the motions which brain substance makes!

But thought is not in the brain substance, for brain substance, without life, is quite unintelligent and dead. Thought is in the *Life Principle* which animates the brain; in the Spirit Substance, which is the real you. The brain does not think, *you think* and express your thoughts through the brain.

There is a Spirit Substance which thinks. Just as the Spirit Substance of each of us permeates our body, and thinks and knows in the body, so the Original Spirit Substance, God, permeates all nature and thinks and knows in nature. *Nature is as intelligent as we are, and knows more than us* – Nature knows all things. The All-Mind has been in touch with all things from the beginning, and it contains all knowledge. Human experience covers a few things, and these things we know. But God's experience covers all the things that have happened since the creation, from the wreck of a planet or the passing of a comet to the fall of a sparrow. All that is and all that has been are *present* in the Intelligence which is wrapped about us and enfolds us and presses upon us from every side.

Many people live in the *past*, recalling what was and, are perhaps resentful, how things were; many people live in the *future*, looking ahead and worrying about things that may happen.

- Past – guilt, anger, resentment
- Future – fear, worry, doubt, anxiety

Since past, present, and future are all NOW in Intelligent Substance, those who live in the NOW are aligning themselves with All-Knowledge. Experience the moment of being Whole... being One... being a Thinking Being with All-Knowledge.

All the encyclopedias that have been written are but trivial affairs compared to the vast knowledge held by the Mind in which we live, move, and have our being.

The truths you perceive by *inspiration* are thought held in this Mind. If truths were not thoughts you could not perceive them, for they would have no existence. Truths could not exist as thoughts unless there is a mind for them to exist in; and *a mind can be nothing else than a substance which thinks.*

You are Thinking Substance, a portion of the Cosmic Substance, but you are *limited,* while the Cosmic Intelligence from which you sprang, which Jesus calls the Father, is *unlimited.* All intelligence, power, and force come from the Father. Jesus recognized this and stated it very plainly. Over and over again he ascribed all his wisdom and power to his unity with the Father, and to his perceiving the thoughts of God. "My Father and I are one." This was the foundation of his knowledge and power. He showed the people the necessity of becoming spiritually awakened; of hearing his voice and becoming like him.

He compared the unthinking human who is the prey and sport of circumstance to the dead man in a tomb, and begged us to hear and come forward. "God is spirit," Jesus said, "be born again, become spiritually awake, and you may see His kingdom. Hear my voice; see what I am and what I do, and come forth and live. The words I speak are spirit and life; accept them and they will cause a well of water to spring up within you. Then you will have life within yourself."

All the encyclopedias that have been written are but trivial affairs compared to the vast knowledge held by the Mind in which we live, move, and have our being.

"I do what I see the Father do," he said, meaning that he read the thoughts of God. "The Father shows all things to the son." "If any man has the will to do the will of God, he will know truth." "My teaching is not my own, but His who sent me." "You will know the truth and the truth will make you free." "The Spirit will guide you into all truth."

The prophets and seers and great men and women, past and present, were made great by what wisdom they received from God, not by what they were taught by other people.

SUMMARY

You too can read the thoughts of the Higher Power. We are immersed in Mind and that Mind contains all knowledge and all truth. It is seeking to give us this knowledge, for our Father-Mother delights to give good gifts to us. The prophets and seers and great men and women, past and present, were made great by what wisdom they received from God, not by what they were taught by other people.

This limitless reservoir of wisdom and power is open to you – you can draw upon it as you will, according to your needs.

- You can make yourself what you desire to be.
- You can do what you wish to do.
- You can have what you want.

To accomplish this you must learn to become one with the Father-Mother –

- so that you may perceive truth;

- so that you may have wisdom and know the right ends to seek and the right means to use to attain those ends, and;

- so that you may secure power and ability to use the means.

In closing this chapter, resolve that you will now put aside all else and concentrate upon the attainment of *conscious unity with the Source.*

It is a great thing to love humanity so, and it is only achieved by thought. Nothing can make you great but thought. Excellent philosophers throughout history have given great thought to genius:

"We may divide thinkers into those who think for themselves and those who think through others. The latter are the rule and the former the exception. The first are original thinkers in a double sense, and egotists in the noblest meaning of the word."

–Schopenhauer

"The key to every man is his thought. Sturdy and defiant though he look, he has a helm which he obeys, which is the idea after which all his facts are classified. He can only be reformed by showing him a new idea which commands his own." *–Emerson*

"Some people study all their lives, and at their death they have learned everything except to think." *–Domergue*

CHAPTER FIVE

STEP 1: MIND & BODY PREPARATION

"Draw nearer to God and He will draw nearer to you."

If you become like the Creator, you can read His thoughts, and if you do not you will find the inspirational perception of truth impossible. *You can never become a great man or woman until you have overcome anxiety, worry, and fear.* It is impos-

You can never become a great man or woman until you have overcome anxiety, worry, and fear.

sible for an anxious person, a worried one, or a fearful one to perceive truth. All things are distorted and thrown out of their proper relations by such mental states, and those who are in them cannot read the thoughts of Higher Intelligence.

If you are poor, or if you are anxious about business or financial matters, you are recommended to study carefully the first volume of this series, *The Science of Getting Rich.* It will present to you a solution for your problems of this nature, no matter how large or how complicated they may seem to be. There is not the least cause for worry about financial affairs. Every person who wills to do so can rise above want, have all they need, and become rich. The same Source from which you will receive mental unfoldment and spiritual power is at your service for the supply of all your material wants. Study this truth until it is fixed in your thoughts and until anxiety is banished from your mind; enter *the Certain Way*, which leads to material riches.

Again, if you are anxious or worried about your health, realize it is possible for you to attain perfect health so that you can have strength sufficient for all that you wish to do and more. That Intelligence which stands ready to give you wealth and mental and spiritual power will rejoice to give you health also. Read the third volume of this series, *The Science of Well-Being*, and know that perfect health is yours for the asking, if you will only obey the simple laws of life and live right. Conquer ill health and eliminate fear.

But it is not enough to rise above financial and physical anxiety and worry, you must rise above moral wrong-doing as well. Scan your inner consciousness now for the motives which motivate you, and make sure they are right.

✸ 1. You must *release all lust*, and cease to be ruled by appetite. You must begin to govern appetite, and eat only to satisfy hunger, never for gluttonous pleasure. And in all things you must make the body obey the spirit.

✷ 2. *You must abandon greed.* Have no unworthy motive in your desire to become rich and powerful. It is legitimate and right to desire riches, if you want them for the sake of the soul, but not if you desire them for the lusts of the body.

✷ 3. *Let go of pride and vanity.* Have no thought of trying to rule over others or of outdoing them. This is a vital point: there is no temptation so insistent as the selfish desire to rule over others. Nothing so appeals to the average man or woman as to sit in the uppermost places at banquets, to be respectfully acknowledged in public, and to be called Rabbi, Master, Sir-Madam. To exercise some sort of control over others is the secret motive of every selfish person. The struggle for power over others is the battle of the *competitive world*, and you must rise above that world and its motives and aspirations and *seek only for life!*

✸ 4. *Dismiss envy.* You can have all that you want, and you need not envy anyone what they have. Above all things, see to it that you *do not hold malice or animosity* toward anyone; to do so cuts you off from the Mind whose treasures you seek to make your own. "If you do not love your fellow being, you do not love the Creative One." Put aside all narrow personal ambition and determine to seek the highest good, and to be swayed by no unworthy selfishness.

SUMMARY

Go over all the vices and get these moral temptations out of your heart one by one — determine to keep them out! Then resolve that you will not only abandon all wrong thought, but that you will eliminate all deeds, habits, and courses of action which will keep you from your highest ideals. This is supremely important, because by doing so you vicariously overcome fear, worry, and anxiety about not doing the right thing. You will live morally correct and thus be able to read the thoughts of Intelligence. Make this resolution of correctness with all the power of your soul, and you are ready for the next step toward greatness and excellence, which you will find explained in the following chapter.

CHAPTER SIX

STEP 2: EVOLVING SOCIAL AND INDIVIDUAL VIEWPOINTS

"*Without faith it is impossible to please Spirit,*" and without faith it is impossible for you to reach excellence.

The distinguishing characteristic of all really great men and women is an unwavering faith. We see this in Joan of Arc in her unending quest to free France; we see it in Churchill during the dark days of World War II; we see it in Ted Turner,

You must learn to see the world as being produced by evolution, as a something which is evolving and becoming, not as a finished work.

Chairman of the Board of CNN, bringing global news to every corner of the world, when people said that it "can't be done" – we see it in every man and woman who has attained a place on the roster of the great ones of the world.

Faith, not a faith in one's self or in one's own power, but faith in Principle; in the Something Great which upholds right, and which may be relied upon to give us the victory in due time. Without this faith it is not possible for anyone to rise to real excellence. The person who has no faith in Principle will always be a small person. Whether you have this faith or not depends upon your point of view. *You must learn to see the world as being produced by evolution, as a something which is evolving and becoming, not as a finished work.*

Millions of years ago the Supreme worked with very low and crude forms of life, yet each was perfect after its kind. Higher and more complex organisms, animal and vegetable, appeared through the successive ages. The earth passed through stage after stage in its unfoldment, each stage perfect in itself, and to be succeeded by a higher one. What we wish you to note is that the so-called "lower organisms" are as perfect after their kind as the higher ones; that the world in the Eocene period was perfect for that period — it was perfect, but the Spirit's work was not finished. This is true of the world today. Physically, socially, and industrially it is all good, and it is all perfect. It is not complete anywhere or in any part, but so far as the handiwork of God has done, it is perfect.

THIS MUST BE YOUR POINT OF VIEW: THAT THE WORLD AND ALL IT CONTAINS IS PERFECT, THOUGH NOT COMPLETED.

"All is right with the world." That is the great fact. There is nothing wrong with anything; there is nothing wrong with anybody. All the facts of life you must contemplate from this standpoint. There is nothing wrong with Nature. Nature is a great *advancing presence,* working beneficently for the happiness of all. All things in Nature are good; she has no evil. She is not complete, for creation is still unfinished, but she is going on to give to

Perceive society, government, and industry, as being perfect now, and as advancing rapidly toward being complete.

us even more bountifully than she has given to us in the past. *Nature is a partial expression of the Source, and Source is love. She is perfect but not complete.*

So true of human society and government, though there are industrial monopolies and conglomerates of capital, strikes, and lockouts. All these things are part of the forward movement; they are incidental to the evolutionary process of completing society. When it is complete, there will be no more of these inharmonies, but it cannot be completed without them. Rockefeller was as necessary to the coming social order as the strange animals of the age of reptiles were to the life of the succeeding period. And just as these animals were perfect after their kind, so Rockefeller was perfect after his kind. Behold, it is all very good!

Perceive society, government, and industry, as being perfect now, and as advancing rapidly toward being complete. You will then understand that there is nothing to fear, no cause for anxiety, nothing to worry about. Never complain of any of these things. They are perfect; *this is the very best possible world for the stage of development humans have reached.*

This notion of perfection will sound like foolishness to many, perhaps to most people. "What!" they will say, "are not child labor and the exploitation of land, in Third World countries, of men and women in filthy and unsanitary conditions evil things? Are not bars or drug houses evil? Do you mean to say that we should accept all these and call them good?"

Child labor and similar things are no more evil than the way of living and the habits and practices of the cave-dweller were evil. Their ways were those of the savage stage of human growth, and for that stage they were perfect. The world's industrial practices are those of the savage stage of industrial development, and they are also perfect. Nothing better is possible until we cease to be *mental* savages in industry and business, and become men and women. This can only come about by the rise of the whole race to a higher viewpoint. And this can only come about by the rise of such individuals here and there as are ready for the higher viewpoint, as can be witnessed now in many of the developed countries.

The cure for all these inharmonies lies not with the upper echelons or employers, but with the workers themselves. Whenever they reach a higher viewpoint, whenever they will desire to do so, they can establish complete brotherhood and harmony in industry – they have the numbers and the power. They are getting now what they desire. Whenever they desire more in the way of a higher, purer, more harmonious life, they will receive more.

True, they want more now, but they only want more of the things that make for animal enjoyment, and so industry remains in the savage, brutal, animal stage. When the workers begin to rise to the mental plane of living, and ask for more of the things that make a better life for the mind and soul, industry will at once be raised above the plane of savagery, brutality and competition. This process can be witnessed now in our tumultuous world. There is always strife as the masses mentally and physically adjust to their inner choice for evolution – higher living. But it is perfect now upon its plane. Behold, it is all very good.

So too of bars and crack houses. If a majority of the people desire these things, it is right and necessary that they should have them. When a majority desires a world without discord, they will create a world in which there exists a constant – "winds of change." So long as men and women are on the plane of bestial thought, so too will the social order be in part disorder, and will show bestial manifestations. The people make society what it is, and as the people rise above the bestial thought, society will rise above the beastly in its manifestations. But a society which thinks in a lowly way must have bars and dives; it is perfect after its kind, as the world was in the Paleogene period, and as it should be.

You can work to complete an unfinished society, instead of trying to renovate a decaying one – and you can work with a better heart and a more hopeful spirit.

All this does not prevent you from working for better things. *You can work to complete an unfinished society, instead of trying to renovate a decaying one – and you can work with a better heart and a more hopeful spirit.* It will make an immense difference with your faith and spirit whether you look upon civilization as a good thing which is becoming better or as a bad and evil thing which is decaying!

* One viewpoint gives you an advancing and expanding mind, and the other gives you a descending and decreasing mind.

* One viewpoint will make you grow greater, and the other will inevitably cause you to grow smaller.

* One will enable you to work for the eternal things, to do large works in an excellent way, toward the completing of all that is incomplete and inharmonious; and the other will make you a mere patch-work-reformer, working almost without hope to save a few lost souls from what you will grow to consider as a lost and doomed world.

SUMMARY

Besides being vitally important, the matter of your evolving social point of view, is one which is likely to give you the most challenge to becoming excellent (so we have driven home the idea here in this chapter).

We have been trained, partly by mistaken religious teachers and doom-and-gloom prophets, to look upon the world as being like a wrecked ship, storm-driven upon a rocky coast; utter destruction is inevitable at the end, and the most that can be done is to rescue, perhaps, a few of the crew. This view teaches us to consider the world as essentially bad and growing worse; and to believe that existing discords and injustices must continue and intensify until the end. It robs us of hope for society, government, and humanity, and gives us a decreasing outlook and contracting mind.

This is all wrong. The world is not wrecked. It is like a magnificent cruise ship with the engines in place and the machinery in perfect order. The tanks are full of oil, and the ship is amply provisioned for the journey; there is no lack of any good thing. Every provision Omniscience could devise has been made for the safety, comfort, and happiness of the crew; the ship is out on the high seas tacking here and there because no one has yet learned the right course to steer. We are learning to steer, and in due time will come magnificently into the harbor of perfect harmony.

The world is good, and growing better. Existing discords and injustices are but the rolling of the ship incidental to our own imperfect steering; they will all be removed in due time. This view gives us an increasing outlook and an expanding mind; it enables us to think largely of society and of ourselves, and to do things in a great way.

It makes a vast difference to you, this matter of the social viewpoint, if you think:

> *"All is right with the world. Nothing can possibly be wrong but my personal attitude, and I will make that right. I will see the facts of nature and all the events, circumstances, and conditions of society, politics, government, and industry from the highest viewpoint. It is all perfect, though incomplete. It is all the handiwork of the Supreme. Behold, it is all very good."*

EVOLVING THE INDIVIDUAL VIEWPOINT

Although it is important how you perceive the facts for social life, it is of less importance than your viewpoint for your fellow beings; for your acquaintances, friends, relatives, your immediate family, and most of all, yourself. You must learn not to look upon the world as a lost and decaying thing but as a something perfect and glorious, which is going on to a most beautiful completeness.

And you must also learn to see men and women not as lost and accursed things, but as perfect beings advancing to become complete. There are no "bad" or "evil" people. An engine which is on the rails pulling a heavy train is perfect after its kind, and it is good. The power of a diesel engine which drives it is good. Let a broken rail throw the engine into the ditch, and it does not become bad or evil by being so displaced; it is a perfectly good engine, but off the track. The power of the diesel engine which drives it into the ditch and wrecks it is not evil, but a perfectly good power. So that which is misplaced or applied in an incomplete or partial way is not evil. There are no evil people; there are perfectly good people who are off the track, but they do not need condemnation or punishment; they only need to get upon the rails again.

That which is undeveloped or incomplete often appears to us as evil, because of the way we have trained ourselves to think. The root of a bulb which will produce a white lily is an unsightly thing; one might look upon it with disgust. But how foolish we would be to condemn the bulb for its appearance, when we know the lily is within it. The root is perfect after its kind; it is a perfect but incomplete lily. And so we must learn to look upon every man, woman, and child (no matter how unlovely in outward manifestation), they are perfect in their stage of being and they are becoming complete. Behold, it is all very good.

Once we come into a comprehension of this fact and arrive at this point of view, we lose all desire to find fault with people, to judge them, criticize them, or condemn them. We no longer work as those who are saving lost souls, but as those who are among the angels, working out the completion of a glorious heaven. We have noth-

> *There are no evil people; there are perfectly good people who are off the track, but they do not need condemnation or punishment; they only need to get upon the rails again.*

ing but good words to say. *It is all good... a great and glorious humanity coming to completeness.*

And in our association with people this puts us into an *expansive and enlarging* attitude of mind. We see them as great beings, and we begin to deal with them and their affairs in a great way. But if we fall to the other point of view, and see a lost and degenerate race, we shrink into the *contracting* mind; and our dealings with humanity and their affairs will be in a small contracted way. Remember to hold steadily to this point of view — if you do you will begin at once to deal with your acquaintances and neighbors and with your own family as a great personality deals with people. This same viewpoint must be the one from which you regard yourself.

We must adjust our point of view and see that nothing can be wrong with our world or with any part of it, including our own affairs. If it is all moving on toward completion, then it is not going wrong; and as our own personal affairs are a part of the whole, they are not going wrong. You and all that you are concerned with are moving on toward completeness. Nothing can check this forward movement but yourself; and you can only check it by assuming a mental attitude which is at cross purposes with the mind of the Supreme. *You have nothing to keep right but yourself; if you keep yourself right, nothing can possibly go wrong with you, and you can have nothing to fear.* No business or other disaster can come upon you if your personal attitude is right, for *you are a part of that which is increasing and advancing, and you must increase and advance with it.*

Moreover your thoughts will be mostly shaped according to your viewpoint of the cosmos. If you see the world as a lost and ruined thing you will see yourself as a part of it, and as partaking of its wrongdoings and weaknesses. *If your outlook for the world as a whole is hopeless, your outlook for yourself cannot be hopeful.* If you see the world as declining toward its end, you cannot see yourself as advancing. Unless you think well of all the works of Intelligence you cannot really think well of yourself, and unless you think well of yourself you can never become great.

SUMMARY

See nature as a great living and advancing presence, and see human society in exactly the same way. It is all one, coming from One Source, and it is all good. You, yourself, are made of the same stuff as Intelligence. All the constituents of the Supreme are parts of yourself; every power that It has is a constituent of human beings. You can move forward as you see God doing. You have within yourself the Source of every power.

As for your individual viewpoint, you must always see yourself as a great advancing soul. Do not dwell upon your faults or condemn your life. Change your attitude about yourself – you are a human "becoming." Learn to say:

"There is THAT in me of which I am made, which knows no imperfection, weakness, or sickness. The world is incomplete, but Cosmic Intelligence in my own consciousness is both perfect and complete. Nothing can be wrong but my own personal attitude, and my own personal attitude can be wrong only when I disobey THAT which is within. I am

a perfect manifestation of Cosmic Intelligence so far as I have gone, and I will press on to be complete. I will trust and not be afraid."

When you are able to say this with understanding, you will have lost all fear, and you will be far advanced upon the road to the development of a great and powerful personality.

CHAPTER SEVEN

STEP 3: CONSECRATION: OBEDIENCE TO YOUR SOUL

Having attained to the viewpoint which puts you into the right relations with the world and with your fellow men and women, the next step is consecration. And *consecration* in its true sense simply means *obedience to the soul.* You have that within you which is ever-impelling you toward the upward and Advancing Way — and that impelling something is the *Divine Principle of Power.*

You must obey it without question. No one will deny the statement that if you are to be great, the excellence must be a manifestation of something within; and that this Something must be the very greatest and highest that is within.

It is not your mind, nor your intellect, nor your reason; you cannot be great if you go no farther back for Principle than to your reasoning power. *Reason knows neither principle nor morality. Your reason is like a lawyer in that it will argue for either side.* Intellect helps us to see the best means and manner of doing the right thing, but intellect never shows us the right thing to do. The intellect of a thief will plan robbery and murder as readily as the intellect of a saint will plan a great philanthropy!

Intellect and reason serve the selfish person for their selfish ends as readily as they serve the unselfish individual for their unselfish ends. Use intellect and reason without regard to Principle, and you may become known as a very able person, but you will never become known as a person whose life shows the power of real genius.

There is too much training in our world of the intellect and reasoning powers, and too little training in obedience to the soul. This is the only thing that can be wrong with your personal attitude – when it fails to be one of obedience to the *Principle of Power.*

> *To be excellent and to have power it is only necessary to conform your life to the pure idea as you find it in the GREAT WITHIN.*

By going back to your own center, you can always find the pure idea of right for every relationship. To be excellent and to have power it is only necessary to conform your life to the pure idea as you find it in the GREAT WITHIN. Every compromise on this point is made at the expense of a loss of power. These six thoughts you *must* remember.

✸ 1. There are many *ideas in your mind* which you have outgrown, and which, from force of habit, you still permit to dictate the actions of your life. Cease all this; abandon everything you have outgrown.

✸ 2. Do not indulge in *distrustful fears* that things will go wrong, or that people will betray you, or mistreat you. Get above all of them.

⁕ 3. You have perhaps formed some *sensual habits* of mind or body. Abandon them.

⁕ 4. There are many *common customs*, social and otherwise, which you still follow, although you know they tend to dwarf and belittle you and keep you acting in a small way. Rise above all this. We are not saying that you should absolutely disregard conventionalities, or the commonly accepted standards of right and wrong. You cannot do this. But you can deliver your soul from most of the narrow restrictions which bind the majority of society.

⁕ 5. Do not give your time and strength to the support of *obsolete institutions*, religious or otherwise; do not be bound by creeds in which you do not believe. Be free.

⁕ 6. You still act selfishly in many ways and on many occasions. Cease to do so.

> *You are a god in the company of gods and must conduct yourself accordingly.*

Abandon all of these, and in place of them put forward the best actions you can; form a conception in your mind. If you desire to advance, and you are not doing so, remember that it can be only because your thought is better than your practice. *You must ACT as well as you THINK!*

- Let your thoughts be ruled by Principle, and then live up to your thoughts.
- Let your attitude in business, in politics, in community affairs, and in your own home be the expression of the best thoughts you can think.
- Let your manner toward all men, women, and children, great and small, and especially to your own family circle, always be the most kindly, gracious, and courteous you can picture in your imagination and act in reality.
- Remember your new viewpoint: *You are a god in the company of gods and must conduct yourself accordingly.*

SUMMARY

The steps to complete consecration or obedience to your soul, are few and simple. You cannot be ruled from below if you are to be great; *you* must rule from above. Therefore, you cannot be governed by physical impulses.

> ✸ 1. You must bring your body into subjugation to your mind; but your mind, without Principle, may lead you into selfishness and immoral ways.
>
> ✸ 2. You must put your mind into subjugation to your soul, and your soul is limited by the boundaries of your knowledge.
>
> ✸ 3. You must put your soul into subjugation to that *Oversoul* which needs no searching for the understanding, but before whose wisdom all things are open. That constitutes consecration. Obey your soul!

Say: "*I surrender my body to be ruled by my mind; I surrender my mind to be governed by my soul, and I surrender my soul to the guidance of Divine Principle.*"

Make this vow complete and thorough, and you have taken the third great step in the way of excellence and power.

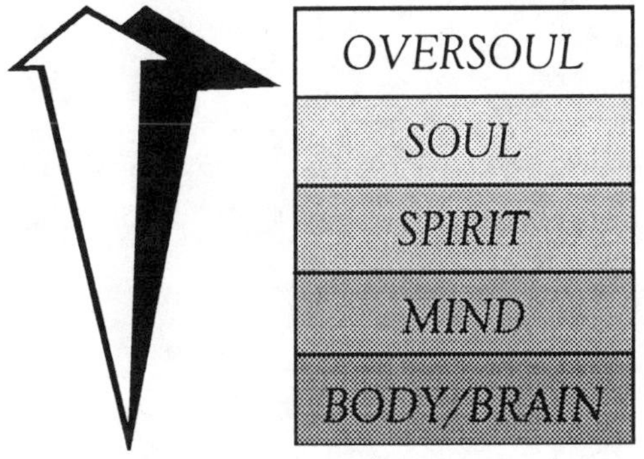

CHAPTER EIGHT

STEP 4: IDENTIFICATION WITH THE SOURCE

Having recognized Spirit as the Advancing Presence in nature, society, and all of humanity, and having harmonized yourself with all these, and having consecrated yourself to that within you which impels toward the greatest and the highest, the fourth step is to become aware of and recognize fully the fact that the *Principle of Power* within you is the Supreme Itself. You must *con-*

sciously identify yourself with the Highest. This is not some false or untrue position to be assumed; it is a *fact* to be recognized. You are already one with the Infinite Source; you now want to become *consciously aware* of it.

You are already one with the Infinite Source; you now want to become consciously aware of it.

There is One Substance, the Source of all things, and this Substance has within Itself the power which creates all things; all power is inherent in It. This Substance is conscious and thinks; It works with perfect understanding and intelligence. You know this to be true because you know that substance exists and that consciousness exists; and that it must be substance which is conscious. We are conscious and think; we are substance. We must be substance, or else we are nothing and do not exist at all.

If you are substance and think, and are conscious, then you are *Conscious Substance.* It is not conceivable that there should be more than one Conscious Substance; so you are the Original Substance, the source of all life and power *embodied in a physical form.* You cannot be something different from God. Intelligence is one and the same everywhere, and must be everywhere as an attribute of the same substance. There cannot be one kind of intelligence in the Source and another kind of intelligence in humans; intelligence can only be within Intelligent Substance, and *Intelligent Substance is God.*

> *...while we are Original Substance, and have within us all power and possibilities, our consciousness is limited.*

We are one stuff with the Infinite, and so all the talents, powers, and possibilities that are in God are in us; not in a few exceptional people, but in everyone. "All power is given to man, in heaven and on earth." "Is it not written, you all are gods?" The *Principle of Power* in you is you yourself, and you are God.

But while we are Original Substance, and have within us all power and possibilities, our *consciousness* is limited. We do not know all there is to know, and so we are liable to error and make mistakes. To save yourself from these you must unite your mind to That outside you which does know all; *you must become consciously one with God.*

✱ *FACT*: There is a Mind surrounding you on every side, closer than breathing, nearer than hands and feet.

✱ *FACT*: And in this Mind is the memory of all that has ever happened, from the greatest upheavals of nature in times past to the fall of a tree in this present time.

✱ *FACT*: Held in this Mind is the *great purpose which is behind all nature,* and so It knows what is going to be.

You are surrounded by a Mind which knows all there is to know... past, present, and future. Everything that humans have said or done or written is stored there. We are of one identical stuff with this Mind; we proceeded from It, and we can so identify ourselves with It that we can know what It knows. "My Father is greater than I," said Jesus, "I come from Him." "I and my Father are one. He shows the son all things." "The Spirit will guide you into all truth."

SUMMARY

The identification of yourself with the Infinite must be accomplished by *conscious recognition on your part.* Recognizing it as a fact, that there is only One, and that all intelligence is in the One Substance, you must affirm:

> *"There is only One and that One is everywhere. I surrender myself to conscious unity with the Highest; not I, but the Source. I will to be one with the Supreme and lead the divine life. I am one with Infinite Consciousness; there is but One Mind, and I am that Mind. I who say these words am One."*

If you have been thorough in the practice as outlined in the preceding chapters... if you have attained to the true viewpoint, and if your obedience to your soul is complete, you will not find conscious identification difficult to attain. And once it is attained, the power you seek is yours, for you have made yourself One with All-Power.

CHAPTER NINE

STEP 5: IDEALIZATION OF YOUR THOUGHT-FORMS

You are a thinking center in Original Substance, and the thoughts of Original Substance have creative power. Whatever is formed in Its thought and held as a thought-form must come into existence as a visible and so-called material form. A thought-form held in Thinking Substance is a reality; it is a real thing, whether it has yet become visible to human eyes or not.

...a thought held in thinking substance is a real thing; a form, and has actual existence, although it is not visible to you.

This is a fact that you should impress upon your understanding—that *a thought held in thinking substance is a real thing; a form, and has actual existence, although it is not visible to you.* You internally take the form in which you think of yourself; and you surround yourself with the invisible forms of those things with which you associate in your thoughts.

If you desire a thing, picture it clearly and hold the picture steadily in mind until it becomes a *definite* thought-form... not just a fleeting thought. And if your daily actions are not such as to separate you from the Source, the thing you want will come to you in material form. It *must* do so in obedience to the law by which the universe was created.

Make no thought-form of yourself in connection with disease or sickness, but form a visualization of perfect health with a high energy level. *Make a thought-form of yourself as strong and hearty and perfectly well.* Impress this thought-form on

Creative Intelligence, and if your habits and actions are not in violation of the laws by which the physical body is built, your thought-form will become manifest in your body. This also is certain; it comes by obedience to law.

Make a thought-form of yourself as you desire to be, and set your ideal as near to perfection as your imagination is capable of forming the visualization.

To illustrate: If a young law student wishes to become great, let them picture themselves (while attending to the viewpoint, consecration, and identification, as previously directed) as a great lawyer, pleading their case with matchless eloquence and power before the judge and jury; as having an unlimited command of truth, of knowledge, and of wisdom. Let them picture themselves as the great lawyer in every possible situation and contingency. While they are still only the student in all circumstances, let them never forget or fail to be the great lawyer in their thought-form of themselves. As the thought-form grows more definite and habitual in their mind, the creative energies, both within and without, are set at work. They begin to manifest the form from within; and all the essentials without, which go into the picture, begin to be impelled toward them. They make themselves into the image and Intelligence works with them; nothing can prevent them from becoming what they wish to be.

In the same general way the musical student pictures themselves as performing perfect harmonies, and as exciting vast audiences; the actor forms the highest conception they are capable of in regard to their art, and applies this conception to themselves. The politician, teacher, artist, farmer, mechanic and the parent do exactly the same thing.

Fix upon your ideal of what you wish to make of yourself. Consider well and be sure that you make the right choice; that is, the one which will be the most satisfactory to *you* in a general way.

> ✷ Do not pay too much attention to the advice or suggestions of those around you; do not believe that anyone can know, better than yourself, what is right for you. Listen to what others have to say, but always form your own conclusions.

DO NOT LET OTHER PEOPLE DECIDE WHAT YOU ARE TO BE. BE WHAT YOU FEEL YOU WANT TO BE.

> *Be true to yourself, and you cannot then be false to anyone.*

✸ Do not be misled by a false notion of obligation or duty. You can owe no possible obligation or duty to others which should prevent you from making the most of yourself. *Be true to yourself, and you cannot then be false to anyone.* When you have fully decided what thing you want to be, form the *highest* conception of that thing that you are capable of imagining, and make that visualization a thought-form. Hold that thought-form as a fact, as the real truth about yourself, and believe in it!

✸ Do not listen to all adverse suggestions; close your heart and mind to them. Never mind if people call you a fool and a dreamer... dream on! Remember that Napoleon Bonaparte, the half-starved lieutenant, always saw himself as the general of armies and the master of France, and he became an outward realization of what he held himself to be in mind. So likewise you, too, will become what you intend your heart and mind towards.

SUMMARY

To your own heart be true. If you are unaware of your great desires, or you do not know what profession to pursue... then listen to Higher Intelligence through meditation, prayer and through your dreams. Work with the Source in building your character. Then hold on to your vision, the thought-form, and formalize your picture in full detail, encompassing the physical, mental and emotional aspects. Adhere carefully to all that has been said in the preceding chapters, and act as directed in the following ones, and you will become what you want to be.

CHAPTER TEN

STEP 6: REALIZATION — BREATHE LIFE INTO SMALL ACTIONS

If you were to stop with the close of the last chapter, however, you would never become great... you would be indeed a mere dreamer of dreams, a castle-builder. Too many do stop there; they do not understand the necessity for *present action* in realizing the vision and bringing the thought-form into manifestation. Two things are necessary.

✷ STEP 1: the making of the thought-form;

✷ STEP 2: the actual appropriation to yourself of all that goes into and around the thought-form. We have discussed the first, now we will proceed to give directions for the second.

When you have made your thought-form, you are already, in your interior, what you want to be; next you must become *externally* what you want to be. You already possess excellence within, but you are not yet doing the excellent things without. You cannot instantly begin to do the great things; you cannot be before the world the great actor, or lawyer, or musician, or personality you know yourself to be. No one will entrust great things to you as yet, for you have not made yourself known... you have not "paid your (physical) dues." But you can always *begin to do small things in an excellent way.*

Here lies the whole secret. You can begin to be great today in your own home, in your store or office, on the street, everywhere. You can begin to make yourself known as great, and you can do this by doing *everything you do in a great way*. You must put the whole power of your great soul into every act, however small and commonplace, and so reveal to your family, your friends, and neighbors what you really are.

✸ *Do not brag or boast of yourself*; do not go about telling people what an excellent person you are; simply live in a great way. No one will believe you if you tell them you are a great individual, but no one can doubt your excellence if you show it in your actions. In your domestic circle be so just, so generous, so courteous, and kindly that your family, your wife, husband, children, brothers, and sisters will know that you are a great and noble soul. In all your relations with people be great, just, generous, courteous, and kind. The great are never otherwise.

✸ Next, and most important, *you must have absolute faith in your own perceptions of truth*. Never act in haste or hurry; be

...all things and events are equal; there is no comparison of great or small in the All-Mind.

deliberate in everything... wait until you feel that you know the true way. And when you do feel that you know the true way, be guided by your own faith although all the world may disagree with you. If you do not believe what Higher Intelligence tells you in little things, you will never draw upon wisdom and knowledge in larger things!

When you sincerely feel that a certain act is the right act, do it and have perfect faith that the consequences will be good. When you are deeply impressed that a certain thing is true, no matter what the appearances to the contrary may be, accept that thing as true and act accordingly.

The one way to develop a perception of truth in large things is to absolutely trust your present perception of truth in small things. Remember that you are seeking to develop this very power or faculty — the perception of truth. You are learning to read the thoughts of the Infinite! Nothing is great and nothing is small in the sight of Omnipotence — holding the sun in its place, or balancing weather patterns, and counting the numbers of hairs of your head — all things and events are equal; there is no comparison of great or small in the All-Mind. The Source is as much interested in the little matters of everyday life as in the affairs of nations.

You can perceive truth about family and neighborhood affairs as well as about matters of government. And the way to begin is to have perfect faith in the truth in these small matters, as it is revealed to you from day to day. When you feel deeply impelled to take a course which seems contrary to all reason and worldly judgment, take that course. Listen to the suggestions and advice of others, but always do what you feel deeply within to be the true thing to do. Rely with absolute faith, at all times, on your own perception of truth; but be sure that you listen to the Inner Voice — that you do not act in haste, fear, or anxiety.

SUMMARY

Rely upon your perception of truth in all the facts and circumstances of life. If you deeply feel that a certain individual will be in a certain place on a certain day, go there with perfect faith to meet them; they will be there, no matter how unlikely it may seem. If you feel sure that certain people are making certain combinations, or doing certain things, act in the faith that they are doing those things. If you feel sure of the truth of any circumstance or happening, near or distant; past, present, or future, trust in your perception.

You may make occasional mistakes at first because of your imperfect understanding of the within; but you will soon be guided almost invariably right. Soon your family and friends will begin to defer, more and more, to your judgment and to be guided by you. Soon your neighbors and government will be coming to you for counsel and advice. Soon you will be recognized as one who is great in small things, and you will be called upon more and more to take charge of larger things. All that is necessary is to be guided absolutely, in all things, by your Inner Light, your perception of truth. Obey your soul, have perfect faith in yourself. Never think of yourself with doubt or distrust, or as one who makes mistakes. *"If I judge, my judgment is just, for I do not seek honor from men, but from the Father only,"* said Jesus.

CHAPTER ELEVEN

ABANDON HURRY AND LIMITING HABITS

No doubt you have many problems – domestic, social, physical, and financial – which seem to you to be pressing for immediate solution. You have debts which must be paid, or other obligations which must be met; you are unhappily or incompatibly placed, and you feel that something must be done at once. *Do not get into a hurry and act from superficial impulses.* You can trust the Source for the solution of all your personal riddles.

> *...the same Intelligence which is in you is in the things you desire. They are impelled toward you as strongly and decidedly as your desire impels you toward them.*

There is no hurry... there is only One, and all is very well with the world.

There is an invincible power in you, and the same power is also in the things you want. It is bringing them to you and bringing you to them. This is a thought that you must grasp, and hold continuously — that the same Intelligence which is in you is in the things you desire. They are impelled toward you as strongly and decidedly as your desire impels you toward them. The tendency, therefore, of a steadily-held thought must be to bring the things you desire to you and to group them around you. So long as you hold your thought and your faith justly, all must go well. *Nothing can be wrong but your own personal attitude, and that will not be wrong if you trust and are not afraid.*

HURRY is a manifestation of fear; one who has no fears has plenty of time! If you act with perfect faith in your own perceptions of truth, you will never be too late or too early; and nothing will go wrong. If things appear to be going wrong, do not get disturbed in mind; it is only in *appearance, which in itself, is illusion. Nothing can go wrong in this world but yourself; and you can go wrong only by getting into the wrong mental attitude.*

Hurry and fear will instantly cut your connection with the Universal Mind; you will get no power, no wisdom, and no information until you are calm.

Whenever you find yourself getting excited, worried, or into the mental attitude of hurry, sit down and think it over; play a game of some kind, or take a vacation. Take a day off, and everything will be all right when you return. As sure as you find yourself in the mental attitude of haste, you will also know that you are out of the mental attitude of greatness. *Hurry and fear will instantly cut your connection with the Universal Mind; you will get no power, no wisdom, and no information until you are calm.* And to fall into the attitude of hurry will *check the action* of the *Principle of Power* within you. *Fear turns strength to weakness!*

Remember that equilibrium and power are inseparably associated. The calm and balanced mind is the strong and great mind; the hurried and agitated mind is the weak one. Whenever you fall into the mental state of hurry you have lost the right viewpoint; you are beginning to look upon the world, or some part of it, as going wrong. At such times read Chapter Six of this book; consider the fact that this world is perfect, now, with all that it contains. Nothing is going wrong; nothing can be wrong. Be self-assured, be calm, be cheerful; have faith in the Universal.

Next, as to HABIT. It is probable that your greatest difficulty will be to overcome your old habitual ways of thought, and to form new habits. The world is ruled by habit. Kings, tyrants, rulers, and dictators hold their positions solely because the people have come to habitually accept them. Things are as they are only because people have formed the habit of accepting them as they are. When the people change their habitual thought about governmental, social, and industrial institutions, they will change the institutions. Habit rules us all!

Perhaps you have formed, the habit of thinking of yourself as a common person, as one with limited ability, or as being more or less a failure. Whatever you habitually think yourself to be, *that* you are. You must form, NOW, a greater and better habit; you must form a visualization of yourself as a being of limitless power, and habitually think that you are of course, that person.

It is the habitual, not the periodical thought that decides your destiny.

It is the habitual, not the periodical thought that decides your destiny. It will be of no benefit to meditate for a few moments several times a day to affirm that you are great, if during the rest of the day, while you are about your regular business, you think of yourself as not being great. No amount of praying or affirmation will make you excel if you still habitually regard yourself as being small.

The use of prayer, affirmation, and meditation is to change your habit of thought. Any act, mental or physical, repeated often, becomes a habit. The purpose of mental exercise is to repeat certain thoughts over and over again until the thinking of those thoughts becomes constant and habitual. Thoughts we continually repeat become convictions. What you must do is to repeat the new thought to yourself until it is the only way in which you think of yourself.

Furthermore, we see that nothing can be wrong with such a world or with any part of it, including our own affairs. If it is all moving on

> *Habitual thought, and not environment or circumstance, has made you what you are.*

toward completion, then it is not going wrong; and as our own personal affairs are a part of the whole, they are not going wrong. You and all that you are concerned with are moving on toward completeness. Nothing can check this forward movement but yourself; and you can only check it by assuming a mental attitude which is at cross purposes with the mind of God. You have nothing to keep right but yourself; if you keep yourself right, nothing can possibly go wrong with you in business or personal disasters.

Moreover your thought-form will be mostly shaped according to your viewpoint of the cosmos. If you see the world as a lost and ruined thing you will see yourself as a part of it, and as partaking of its limitations and weaknesses. If your outlook for the world is hopeless, your outlook for yourself cannot be hopeful. If you see the world as declining toward its end, you cannot see yourself as advancing. Unless you think well of all the works of Spirit you cannot really think well of yourself, and unless you think well of yourself you can never become great.

We repeat that your place in life, including your material environment, is determined by the thought-form you habitually hold of yourself. When you make a thought-form of yourself you can hardly fail to form in your mind a corresponding environment. If you think of yourself as an incapable, inefficient person, you will think of yourself with poor or cheap surroundings. These thoughts, habitually held, become invisible forms in the surrounding mind-stuff, and are with you continually. In due time, by the regular action of the eternal creative energy, the invisible thought-forms are produced in material-stuff, and you are surrounded by your own thoughts made into material things.

See nature as a great living and advancing presence, and see human society in exactly the same way. It is all one, coming from one source, and it is all good. You yourself are made of the same stuff as God. All the constituents of God are parts of yourself; every power that God has is a constituent of us all. You can move forward as you see Life Principle doing. You have within yourself the source of every power.

SUMMARY

Habitual thought, and not environment or circumstance, has made you what you are. Every person has some Central Idea or thought-form of themselves, and by this idea they classify and arrange all their facts and external relationships. You are classifying your facts either according to the idea that you are a excellent and strong personality, or according to the idea that you are limited, common, or weak. If the latter is the case, you must change your Central Idea. *Get a new mental picture of yourself.*

Do not try to become excellent by repeating mere strings of words or superficial formulas; but repeat over and over the THOUGHT of your own power and ability until you classify external facts, and decide your place by this idea. In another chapter we will illustrate a mental exercise and give further directions on this point.

CHAPTER TWELVE

AWAKEN SINCERE THOUGHT

Excellence is attained only by the thinking of great thoughts. You cannot become great in outward personality until you are great internally; and you cannot be great internally until you THINK. No amount of education, reading, or study can make you extraordinary without thought; and thought can make you noteworthy with very little study. There are altogether too many people who are trying to make something of themselves

> *You are not mentally developed by what you read, but by what you think about regarding what you read.*

by reading books... without thinking; all such will fail. *You are not mentally developed by what you read, but by what you think about regarding what you read.*

Thinking is the hardest and most exhausting of all labor; and that is why many people shrink from it! We have been so created that we are continuously impelled toward thought – we must either think or engage in some activity to escape thought. *The headlong, continuous chase for pleasure in which most people spend all their leisure time is only an effort to escape thought.* If they are alone, or if they have nothing amusing to hold their attention, such as a novel to read or music to hear or a movie to see, they must think; and to escape from thinking they resort to novels, music, movies, and all the endless seductions of entertainment. Most people spend the greater part of their leisure time running away from thought, that is why they are where they are. *You can never move forward until you begin to think.*

Read less and think more! Read about great things and extraordinary people, and think about noteworthy questions and issues. We have, at the present time, few really excellent figures in the political life of our world; our politicians are a petty lot. There is no Kennedy, Churchill, Lincoln, or Roosevelt; no Gandhi, Webster, Jefferson, or Franklin. Why? Because our present diplomats deal only with sordid and petty issues — questions of dollars and cents, of expediency and party success, of material prosperity without regard to ethical right. Thinking along these lines does not bring forth great souls. The statesmen of Lincoln's time and previous times dealt with questions of eternal truth; of human rights and justice. People thought upon great themes; they thought great thoughts, and they became great individuals.

> *Thinking, not just knowledge or information, makes personality. Thinking is growth; you cannot think without growing.*

Thinking, not just knowledge or information, makes personality. Thinking is growth; you cannot think without growing. Every thought propagates another thought. Write one idea and others will follow until you have written a page. You cannot fathom your own mind; it has neither bottom nor boundaries. Your first thoughts may be crude; but as you go on thinking you will use more and more of yourself... *you will quicken new brain cells into activity and you will develop new faculties.* Heredity, environment, circumstance—all things must give way before you if you practice *sustained and continuous* thought. But, on the other hand, if you neglect to think for yourself and only use other people's thoughts, you will never know what you are capable of; and you will end up being incapable of anything.

There can be no real greatness without original thought. All that you do outwardly is the expression and completion of your inward thinking. No action is possible without thought, and no superb action is possible until a great thought has preceded it.

* *Action is the second form of thought.*
* *Personality is the materialization of thought.*
* *Environment is the result of thought.*

Things group themselves or arrange themselves around you according to your thought. There is, to paraphrase Emerson, some Central Idea or conception of yourself by which all the facts of your life are arranged and classified. Change this *Central Idea* and you change the arrangement or classification of all the facts and circumstances of your life. *You have a Core Belief about yourself – through thought, visualization, meditation, and action, you can change this self-belief to one of excellence. You are what you are because you think as you do; you are where you are because you think as you do.* It is time for you to set your mental, physical, and spiritual filing cabinets in excellent order.

You see then the immense importance of thinking about the great essentials written in the preceding chapters. You must not accept them in any shallow way; you must think about them until they are a part of your Central Idea. Go back to the enlightening thought that you live in a perfect world among perfect people, and that nothing can possibly be wrong with you but your own personal attitude. Think about all this until you fully realize the scope of what it means to you. Consider that this is the Supreme's world and that it is the best of all possible worlds; that It has brought the universe thus far in creation by the processes of organic, social, and industrial evolution, and that it is going on to greater completeness and harmony.

Consider that there is one great, perfect, intelligent *Principle of Life and Power,* causing all the changing phenomena of the cosmos. Think about all this until you see that it is true, and until you can comprehend how you should live and act as a citizen of such a perfect whole.

Next, think of the wonderful truth that this great Intelligence is in *you*... it is your own intelligence! It is an Inner Light impelling you toward the right thing and the best thing, the greatest act, and the highest happiness. It is a Principle of Power in you, giving you all the ability and genius there is. It will infallibly guide you to the best if you will submit to it and walk in the Light. Consider what is meant by your *consecration* of yourself when you say, *"I will obey my soul."* This is a sentence of tremendous meaning; it must revolutionize the attitude and behavior of the average person.

Then think of your *identification* with this Great Supreme; that all Its knowledge is yours, and all Its wisdom is yours, for the asking. *You are a god if you think like a god.* If you think like a god you cannot fail to act like a god. Divine thoughts will surely externalize themselves in a divine life. *Thoughts of power will end in a life of power.* Great thoughts will manifest in a great personality. Think earnestly of all this, and then you are ready to ACT.

> *To think great things you must be absolutely sincere; and to be sincere you must know that your intentions are right.*

You will never become great until your own thoughts make you great, and therefore it is of the first importance that you should THINK. You will never do great things in the external world until you think great things in the internal world; and you will never think great things until you think about *truth*; about the verities. *To think great things you must be absolutely sincere; and to be sincere you must know that your intentions are right.* Insincere or false thinking is never great, regardless of how logical and brilliant it may be.

> ✸ *STEP 1*: The first and most important step is to seek the truth about human relations; to know what you ought to be to other people, and what they ought to

be to you. This brings you back to the search for a right viewpoint.

You should study organic and social evolution. Read Darwin and Walter Thomas Mills, and when you read, THINK; think the whole matter over until you see the world of things and human kind in the right way. THINK about what Intelligence is doing until you can SEE what It is doing. To truly think is to internalize information, and to find the truth of the matter.

✷ *STEP 2*: Your next step is to think yourself into the right personal attitude. Your viewpoint tells you what the right attitude is, and obedience to the soul puts you into it. It is only by making a complete consecration of yourself to the Highest that is within you that you can attain to *sincere thinking.*

So long as you know you are selfish in your aims, or dishonest or crooked in any way in your *intentions or practices*, your thinking will be false and your thoughts will have no power. THINK about the way you are doing things; about all your intentions, purposes, and practices, until you know that they are right.

✸ *STEP 3: You* must think yourself one with the Supreme. The fact of one's own complete unity with God is one that no person can grasp without deep and sustained thinking.

Anyone can accept the proposition in a superficial way, but to feel and realize a vital comprehension of it is another matter. It is easy to think of going outside of yourself to meet God, but it is not so easy to think of going *inside yourself* to meet God. You will find God is there, and in the holy of holies of your own soul you may meet Him face to face.

It is a tremendous thing, this fact that *all you need is already within you*; that you do not have to consider how to get the power to do what you want to do or to make yourself what you want to be. You have only to consider how to use the power you already have in the right way. And there is nothing to do but to begin. Use your

...you can see some truth today; live fully up to that and you will see more truth tomorrow.

perception of truth; *you can see some truth today; live fully up to that and you will see more truth tomorrow.*

SUMMARY

To rid yourself of the old false ideas you will have to think a great deal about the value of people – the greatness and worth of a human soul. You must stop looking at human mistakes and look at successes; stop seeing faults and see virtues. You can no longer look upon men and women as lost and ruined beings who are descending into hell; you must come to regard them as shining souls who are ascending toward heaven. It will require some exercise of will power to do this, but this is the legitimate use of the will – to decide what you will think about and how you will think. The function of the will is to direct thought. Think about the good side of men; the lovely, attractive part, and exert your will in refusing to think of anything else in connection with them.

We know of no individual who has attained to so much on this one point as Mother Theresa, humanitarian and recipient of the Nobel Prize for Peace. Mother Theresa reverences humanity. No appeal for help is ever made to her in vain. No one receives from her an unkind or condemnatory word. You cannot come into her presence without being made sensible of her deep and kindly personal interest in you. No one, whether millionaire, grimy working man, or hard-working woman, meets her without receiving the radiant warmth of a sisterly affection that is sincere and true. No homeless child speaks to her on the street without receiving instant and tender recognition. Mother Theresa loves people. This has made her the leading figure in a great movement, the beloved hero of a million hearts, and will give her a deathless name.

CHAPTER THIRTEEN

ACTION AT HOME AND ABROAD

Do not merely think that you are going to become excellent — *think that you are excellent now.* ✸ Do not think that you will begin to act in an excellent way at some future time — begin now. ✸ Do not think that you will act in an excellent way when you reach a different environment — act in an excellent way where you are now. ✸ Do not think that you will begin to act in an excellent way when you begin to deal with excellent things —

begin to deal in an excellent way with small things. ✸ Do not think that you will begin to be excellent when you get among more intelligent people, or among people who understand you better — begin now to deal in an excellent way with the people around you.

If you are not in an environment where there is scope for your best powers and talents you can move in due time; meanwhile, you can be outstanding where you are. H. Ross Perot was as great a person when he was a small-town salesperson as when he is head of a multi-billion dollar network; as a salesman he did common things in a great way, and that made him president of his corporation. Had he waited until he reached the top to begin to be excellent, he would have remained unknown. Heads of state call upon him for counsel; to see the truth and just action to take.

You are not made superior by the location in which you happen to be, nor by the things with which you may surround yourself. You are not made superior by what you receive from others; you can never manifest excellence so long as you depend on others. You will manifest excellence only when you begin to stand alone. Reject all thought of reliance on externals, whether things, books, or people. As Emerson said, "Shakespeare will never be made by the study of Shakespeare." Shakespeare will be made by the thinking of Shakespearean thoughts.

Never mind how the people around you, including those of your own household, may treat you. That has nothing at all to do with your being great; that is, it cannot prevent you from being great. People may neglect you and be unthankful and unkind in their attitude toward you; does that prevent you from being excellent in your manner and attitude toward them? "Your Father," said Jesus, "is kind to the unthankful and the evil." Would Divinity be great if It should go away and sulk because people were unthankful and did not appreciate It? Treat the unthankful and the evil in a great and perfectly kind way, just as Intelligence does.

Do not talk about your superiority; you are really, in essential nature, no greater than those around you. You may have entered upon a way of living and thinking which they have not found yet, but they are perfect on their own plane of thought and action. You are entitled to no special honor or consideration for your excellence. You are a god, and you are among gods. You will fall into the boastful attitude if you see other people's shortcomings and failures and compare them with

Think of yourself as a perfect being among perfect beings, and meet every person as an equal, not as either a superior or an inferior.

your own virtues and successes. And if you fall into the boastful attitude of mind, you will cease to be great, and become small. *Think of yourself as a perfect being among perfect beings, and meet every person as an equal, not as either a superior or an inferior.* Give yourself no airs; extraordinary people never do. Ask no honors and seek for no recognition; honors and recognition will come fast enough if you are entitled to them.

Begin at home. It is a great person who can always be genteel, assured, calm, and perfectly kind and considerate at home. If your manner and attitude in your own family are always the best you can think, you will soon become the one on whom all the others will rely. You will be a tower of strength and a support in time of trouble. You will be loved and appreciated.

At the same time, *do not make the mistake of throwing yourself away in the service of others.* The person of excellence respects themselves; they serve and help, but they are never subservient. You cannot help your family by being a slave to them, or by doing for them those things which by right they should do for themselves. You do a person an injury when you wait on them too much. The selfish and calculating are a great deal better off if their knaving are denied.

SUMMARY

The ideal world is not one where there are a lot of people being waited on by other people; it is a world where everyone waits on themselves. Meet all demands, selfish and otherwise, with perfect kindness and consideration.

- Do not allow yourself to be made a slave to the whims, calculations, or menial desires of any member of your family. To do so is not superior, and it injures the other party.

- Do not become uneasy over the failures or mistakes of any member of your family, and feel that you must interfere.

- Do not be disturbed if others seem to be going wrong, and feel that you must

You are a truly great soul when you can live with those who do things which you do not do, and yet refrain from either criticism or interference.

step in and set them right. Remember, that every person is perfect on their own plane; you cannot improve on the work of Higher Intelligence.

✹ Do not meddle with the personal habits and practices of others, though they are your nearest and dearest; these things are none of your business. Nothing can be wrong but your own personal attitude; make that right and you will know that all else is right.

You are a truly great soul when you can live with those who do things which you do not do, and yet refrain from either criticism or interference. Do the things which are right for you to do, and believe that every member of your family is doing the things which are right for them. Nothing is wrong with anybody or anything; acknowledge that it is all very good.

✷ Do not be enslaved by anyone else, but be just as careful that you do not enslave anyone else to your own notions of what is right.

Think, and think deeply and continuously; be perfect in your kindness and consideration; let your attitude be that of a god among other gods, not among inferior beings. This is the way to be great in your own home.

ACTION ABROAD

The rules which apply to your action at home must apply to your action everywhere. Never forget for an instant that this is a perfect world, and that you are a god among gods. You are as great as the greatest, but all are your equals.

Rely absolutely on your perception of truth. Give trust to the Inner Light rather than to reason, but be sure that your perception comes from the Inner Light. Act in stability and calmness; be still and attend to your Higher Power. Your *identification* of yourself with the All-Mind will give you all the knowledge you need for guidance in any contingency which may arise in your own life or in the lives of others. It is only necessary that you should be supremely calm, and rely upon the eternal wisdom which is within you. If you act in balance and faith, your judgment will always be right, and you will always know exactly what to do.

Do not hurry or worry; remember Lincoln in the dark days of the Civil War. James Freeman Clarke relates that after the battle of Fredericksburg, Lincoln alone furnished a supply of faith and hope for the nation. Hundreds of leading men, from all parts of the country, went sadly into his room and came out cheerful and hopeful. They had stood face to face with the Highest, and had seen Intelligence in this lank, ungainly, patient man, although they did not know it.

Have perfect faith in yourself and in your own ability to cope with any combination of circumstances that may arise.

> ✸ Do not be disturbed if you are alone; if you need friends they will be brought to you at the right time.

> ✸ Do not be disturbed if you feel that you are ignorant; the information that you need will be furnished you when it is time for you to have it. That which is in you impelling you forward is in the things and people you need, impelling them toward you.

> ✸ Do not be disturbed if you do not know where to turn for information. If there is a particular person you need to know, they will be introduced to you; if there is a particular book you need to read, it will be placed in your hands at the right time.

All the knowledge you need will come to you from both *external and internal* sources. Your information and your talents will always be equal to the requirements of the occasion. As soon as you awaken and begin to use your faculties in a superior way you will apply power to the development of your brain; new cells will be created and dormant cells quickened into activity, and *your brain will be qualified as a perfect instrument for your mind.*

* Do not try to do great things until you are ready to go about them in a Great Way. If you undertake to deal with great matters in a small way – that is, from a inferior viewpoint or with incomplete consecration and wavering faith and courage – you will fail.

* Do not be in a hurry to get to the great things. Doing great things will not make you great, but Becoming Excellent will certainly lead you to the doing of great

things. Begin to be great where you are and in the things you do every day.

> *...the joy of being something and of knowing that you are advancing is the greatest of all joys possible to us.*

⁕ Do not be in a hurry to be found out or to be recognized as a great personality.

⁕ Do not be disappointed if people do not nominate you for office within a month after you begin to practice what you read in this book. Great people never seek for recognition or applause; they are not great because they want to be paid for being so. *Greatness is reward enough for itself; the joy of being something and of knowing that you are advancing is the greatest of all joys possible to us.*

If you begin in your own family, as described earlier, and then assume the same mental attitude with your neighbors, friends, and those you meet in business, you will soon find that people are beginning to depend on you. Your advice will be sought, and a constantly increasing number of people will look to you for strength and inspiration, and rely upon your judgment.

Here, as in the home, you must avoid meddling with other people's affairs. Help all who come to you, but do not go about presumptuously endeavoring to set other people right. Mind your own business! It is no part of your mission in life to correct people's morals, habits, or practices. Lead a great life, doing all things with a great spirit and in a Great Way. Give to Him that ask of you as freely as you have received, but do not force your help or your opinions upon any person. If your neighbor wishes to smoke or drink, it is their business; it is none of yours until they consult you about it. If you lead a great life and do no preaching, you will save a thousand times as many souls as one who leads a small life and preaches continuously.

SUMMARY

If you hold the right viewpoint of the world, others will find it out and be impressed by it through your daily conversation and practice. Do not try to convert others to your point of view, except by holding it and living accordingly. If your *consecration* is perfect you do not need to tell anyone; it will quickly become apparent to all that you are guided by a Higher Principle than the average man or woman. If your *identification* with the Supreme is complete, you do not need to explain the fact to others; it will become self-evident. To become known as a great personality, you have nothing to do but to live. Do not imagine that you must go charging about the world like Don Quixote, tilting at windmills, and overturning things in general, in order to demonstrate that you are somebody. Do not go hunting for big things to do. Live a great life where you are, and in the daily work you have to do, and greater works will surely find you out. Big things will come to you, asking to be done.

Be so impressed with the value of a person that you treat even a beggar or the homeless with the most distinguished consideration. All is God. Every man and woman is perfect. Let your manner be that of a god addressing other gods. Do not save all your consideration for the poor; the millionaire is as good as the worker. This is a perfectly good world, and there is not a person or thing in it but is exactly right; be sure that you keep this in mind in dealing with things and people.

Form your mental vision of yourself with care. Make the thought-form of yourself as you wish to be, and hold this with the faith that it is being realized, and with the purpose to realize it completely. Do every common act as a god should do it; speak every word as a god should speak it; meet men and women of both low and high status as a god meets other divine beings. Begin so and continue so, and your unfoldment in ability and power will be great and rapid.

CHAPTER FOURTEEN

A VIEW OF EVOLUTION

How will we avoid throwing ourselves into altruistic work if we are surrounded by poverty, ignorance, suffering, and every appearance of misery as very many people are? Those who live where people have their hands out, coming from every side appealingly for aid must find it hard to refrain from continuous giving. Again, there are social and other irregularities, injustices done to the weak, which fire generous souls with an almost irresistible desire to set things right. We want to start a crusade, a committee; we feel that the wrongs will never be righted until we give ourselves wholly to the task. In all this we must fall back upon the point of view. We must remember that this is not a bad world but a good world in the process of becoming.

Beyond all doubt there was a time when there was no life upon this earth. The testimony of geology to the fact that the globe was once a ball of burning gas and molten rock, surrounded with boiling vapors, is indisputable. And we do not know how life could have existed under such conditions; that seems impossible. Geology tells us that later on a crust formed, the globe cooled and hardened, the vapors condensed and became mist or fell in rain. The cooled surface crumbled into soil; moisture accumulated, ponds and seas were gathered together, and at last somewhere in the water or on the land appeared something that was alive.

It is reasonable to suppose that this first life was in single-celled organisms, but behind these cells was the insistent urge of Spirit, the Great One Life seeking expression. And soon organisms having too much life to express themselves with one cell had two cells and then many, and still more life was poured into them. Multiple-celled organisms were formed; plants, trees, vertebrates, and mammals, many of them with strange shapes, but all were perfect after their kind as everything is... that God makes. No doubt there were crude and almost monstrous forms of both animal and plant life; but everything filled its purpose in its day and it was all very good. Then another day came, the great day of the evolutionary process.

An ape-like being, little different from the beasts around him in appearance but infinitely different in his capacity for growth and thought. Art and beauty, architecture and song, poetry and music, all these were unrealized possibilities in that ape man's soul. And for his time and kind he was very good.

"It is God that works in you to will and to do of his good pleasure," says St. Paul. From the day the first man appeared Consciousness began to work IN human beings, putting more and more of Himself into each succeeding generation, urging them on to larger achievements and to better conditions, social, governmental, and domestic.

Those who looking back into ancient history see the awful conditions which existed, the outsiders, demonism, and sufferings, and reading about the Infinite in connection with these things are disposed to feel that He was cruel and unjust to man, should pause to think. From the ape-man to the coming Christ-man the race has had to rise. And it could only be accomplished by the successive unfoldment of the various powers and possibilities latent in the human brain. Naturally the cruder and more animal-like part of humans came to its full development first. For ages humans were brutal; their governments were brutal, their religions were brutal, their domestic institutions were brutal, and what appears to be an immense amount of suffering resulted from this brutality. But the Source never delighted in suffering, and in every age It has given us a message, telling them how to avoid it. And all the while the urge of life, insistent, powerful, compelling, made the race keep moving forward; a little less brutality in each age and a little more spirituality in each age. And Spirit kept on working in us.

In every age there have been some individuals who were in advance of the mass and who heard and understood God better than their fellow beings. Upon these the inspiring hand of

DATE 07/23/2005 | 015887 CRMN | TIME 16:30:37

MAUI BOOKSELLERS
105 N. MARKET ST 101B
WAILUKU, HI 96793
(808) 244-9091
THANK YOU

CREDIT SALE

TRANS # 003
AUTH # 036558
TRANSID MCWRS6JDB0723

MSTR ACCOUNT #
7956

SALE AMOUNT $23.42

CUSTOMER COPY

DATE	015887	TIME
07/23/2005	CRMN	16:30:37

MAUI BOOKSELLERS
105 N. MARKET ST 101B
WAILUKU, HI 96793
(808) 244-9091
THANK YOU

CREDIT SALE

TRANS # 003
AUTH # 036568
TRANSID MCWR56JD90723

MSTR ACCOUNT #
7956

SALE AMOUNT $23.42

CUSTOMER COPY

Spirit was laid and they were compelled to become interpreters. These were the prophets and seers, and sometimes the priests and kings, and often times still they were martyrs driven to the stake, the block, or the cross. It is to these who have heard All-Mind, spoken Its word, and demonstrated Its truth in their lives that all progress is really due.

> *...that which appears to us to be evil is only undeveloped; and that the undeveloped is perfectly good in its own stage and place*

Again, considering for a moment the presence of what is called evil in the world, we see *that which appears to us to be evil is only undeveloped; and that the undeveloped is perfectly good in its own stage and place.* Because all things are necessary to our complete unfoldment, all things in human life are the work of the Source. The ghettoes in our cities, the red-light districts and their unfortunate inhabitants, these He consciously and voluntarily produced. Their part in the plan of unfoldment must be played. And when their part has been played he will sweep them off the stage as he did the strange and poisonous monsters which filled the swamps of the past ages.

SUMMARY

In concluding this vision of evolution we might ask why it was all done, what is it for? This question should be easy for the thoughtful mind to answer. Infinite desired to express Himself, to live in form, and not only that, but to live in a form through which He could express Himself on the highest moral and spiritual plane. God wanted to evolve a form in which He could live as a god and manifest Himself as a god. This was the aim of the evolutionary force. The ages of warfare, bloodshed, suffering, injustice, and cruelty were tempered in many ways with love and justice as time advanced. And this was developing the brain of man to a point where it should be capable of giving full expression to the love and justice of Source. The end is not yet; Cosmic Intelligence aims not at the perfection of a few choice specimens for exhibition, like the large berries at the top of the grocery container, but at the glorification of the race. The time will come when the Kingdom of Heaven will be established on earth.

CHAPTER FIFTEEN

FAVOR HIGHER INTELLIGENCE

We have brought you so far through the two preceding chapters with a view to finally settling the question of duty. This is one that puzzles and perplexes very many people who are earnest and sincere, and gives them a great deal of difficulty in its solution. When they start out to make something of themselves and to practice the *Science of Being Excellent*, they find themselves necessarily compelled to rearrange many of their relationships.

There are friends who perhaps must be alienated, there are relatives who misunderstand and who feel that they are in some way being slighted; the really great person is often considered selfish by a large circle of people who are connected with them and who feel that they might bestow upon them more benefits than they do. The question at the outset: Is it my duty to make the most of myself regardless of everything else? Or should I wait until I can do so without any friction or without causing loss to anyone? This is the question of duty to self versus duty to others.

One's duty to the world has been thoroughly discussed in the preceding pages and we give some consideration now to the idea of duty to Higher Intelligence. An immense number of people have a great deal of uncertainty, not to say anxiety, as to what they ought to do for Spirit. The amount of work and service that is done for Him in the World by way of church work and so on is enormous. An immense amount of human energy is expended in what is called serving God. We propose to briefly consider what serving God means and how you may serve God best, and to make it plain that the conventional idea as to what constitutes service to God is all wrong.

When Moses went down into Egypt to bring out the Hebrews from bondage, his demand upon Pharaoh, in the name of the Deity, was, "Let the people go that they may serve me." He led them out into the wilderness and there instituted a new form of worship which has led many people to suppose that worship constitutes the service of God, although later God himself distinctly declared that He cared nothing for ceremonies, burned offerings, or oblation, and the teaching of Jesus, if rightly understood, would do away with organized temple worship altogether. Source does not lack anything that we may do for It with their hands or bodies or voices. Saint Paul points out that we can do nothing for God, for God does not need anything.

The view of evolution which we have taken shows the Infinite seeking expression through humankind. Through all the successive ages in which His spirit has urged man up the height, God has gone on seeking expression. Every generation of our species is more Godlike than the preceding generation. Every generation demands more in the way of fine homes, pleasant surroundings, congenial work, rest, travel, and opportunity for study than the preceding generation.

There are shortsighted economists who argue that the working people of today ought surely to be fully contented because their condition is so much better than that of the working man two hundred years ago who slept in a windowless hut on a floor covered with rushes in company with his pigs. If that man had all that he was able to use for the living of all the life he knew how to live, he was perfectly content, and if he had lack he was not contented.

The person of today has a comfortable home and very many things, indeed, that were unknown a short period back in the past, and if they have all that they can use for the living of all the life they can imagine, they will be content. Yet people are not content. We have been lifted so far that any common person can picture a better and more desirable life than they are able to live under existing conditions. And so long as this is true, so long as you can think and clearly picture to yourself a more desirable life, you will be discontented with the life you have to live, and rightly so. That discontent is the Spirit of God urging us on to more desirable conditions. It is Higher Intelligence who seeks expression in the race.

The only service you can render the All-Mind is to give expression to what He is trying to give the world, through you. The only service you can render Mind is to make the very most of yourself in order that Mind may live in you to the utmost of your possibilities. In a former work of this series (*The Science of Getting Rich*), we refer to the little girl at the piano, the music in whose soul could not find expression through her untrained hands. This is a good illustration of the way the Spirit of God is over, about, around, and in all of us, seeking to do great things with us, so soon as we will train our hands and feet, our minds, brains, and bodies to do His service.

Your first duty to God, to yourself, and to the world is to make yourself as great a personality, in every way, as you possibly can. And that, it seems to me, disposes of the question of duty.

SUMMARY

We have said, in a general way, that it is within the power of everyone to become great, just as in *The Science of Getting Rich* we declared that it is within the power of everyone to become rich. But these sweeping generalizations need qualifying. There are people who have such materialistic minds that they are absolutely incapable of comprehending the philosophy written in these books. There is a great mass of men and women who have lived and worked until they are practically incapable of thought along these lines; and they cannot receive *The Science of Getting Rich's* message. Something may be done for them by demonstration, that is, by living the life before them. But that is the only way they can be aroused. *The world needs demonstration more than it needs teaching.* For this mass of people our duty is to become as great in personality as possible in order that they may see and desire to do likewise. It is our duty to make ourselves great for their sakes, so that we may help prepare the world that the next generation will have better conditions for thought.

One other point. Frequently, people write or call who wish to make something of themselves and to move out into the world, but who are hampered by home ties, having others more or less dependent upon them, whom they fear would suffer if left alone. In general, we advise such people to move out fearlessly, and to make the most of themselves. If there is a loss at home it will be only temporary and apparent, for in time, if you follow the leading of Spirit, you will be able to take better care of your dependents than you have ever done before.

CHAPTER SIXTEEN

DAILY THOUGHTS OF EXCELLENCE

The purpose of mental exercises must not be misunderstood. There is no virtue in charms or formulated strings of words; there is no short cut to development by repeating prayers or incantations. A mental exercise is an exercise, not in repeating words, but in the *thinking of certain thoughts.* The phrases that we repeatedly hear become convictions, as Goethe says; and the thoughts that we repeatedly think become habitual, and make us what we are. The purpose in doing a mental exercise is that you may think certain thoughts repeatedly until you form a habit of thinking them; then they will be your thoughts all the time. Taken in the right way and with an understanding of their purpose, mental exercises are of great value; but taken as most people take them they are worse than useless.

The thoughts embodied in the following exercise are the ones you want to think. You should do the exercise once or twice daily, but you should think the thoughts continuously. That is, do not think them twice a day for a stated time and then forget them until it is time to do the exercise again. The exercise is to impress you with the material for continuous thought.

Take time when you can have from fifteen minutes to half an hour secure from interruption, and proceed first to make yourself physically comfortable. Relax in a reclining chair, or on a couch, or in bed; it is best to lie flat on your back. If you have no other time, do the exercise upon going to bed at night and before rising in the morning.

First let your attention travel over your body from the crown of your head to the soles of your feet, relaxing every muscle as you go. Relax completely. And next, get physical illnesses and mental worries off your mind. Let your attention pass down the spinal cord and out over the nerves to the extremities, and as you do so think...

"My nerves are in perfect order all over my body. They obey my will, and I have great nerve force." Next, bring your attention to the lungs and think...

"I am breathing deeply and quietly, and the air goes into every cell of my lungs, which are in perfect condition. My blood is purified and made clean." Next, to the heart...

"My heart is beating strongly and steadily, and my circulation is perfect, even to the extremities." Next, to the digestive system...

"My stomach and intestines perform their work perfectly. My food is digested and assimilated and my body rebuilt and nourished. My liver, kidneys, and bladder each perform their several functions without pain or strain; I am perfectly well. My body is resting, my mind is quiet, and my soul is at peace.

"I have no anxiety about financial or other matters. Intelligence, who is within me, is also in all things I want, impelling them toward me; all that I want is already given to me. I have no anxiety about my health, for I am perfectly well. I have no worry or fear whatever.

"I rise above all temptation. I abandon all greed, selfishness, and narrow personal ambition; I do not hold envy, malice, or hatred toward any living soul. I will follow no course of action which is not in accord with my highest ideals. I am right and I will do right."

VIEWPOINT

"All is right with the world. It is perfect and advancing to completion. I will contemplate the facts of social, political, and industrial life only from this high viewpoint. Behold, it is all very good. I will see all human beings, all my acquaintances, friends, neighbors, and the members of my own household in the same way. They are all good. Nothing is wrong with the universe; nothing can be wrong but my own personal attitude, and from now on I keep that right. My whole trust is in Cosmic Intelligence."

CONSECRATION

"I will obey my soul and be true to that within me which is highest. I will search within for the pure idea of right in all things, and when I find it, I will express it in my outward life. I will abandon everything I have outgrown for the best ideal I can imagine. I will have the highest thoughts concerning all my relationships, and my manner and action will express these thoughts. I surrender my body to be ruled by my mind; I yield my mind to the dominion of my soul, and I give my soul to the guidance of the Supreme."

IDENTIFICATION

"There is but One Substance and Source, and of that I am made, and with it I am one. It is my Father-Mother; I proceeded forth and came from It. My Father-Mother and I are one, and my Father-Mother is greater than I, and I do Its will. I surrender myself to conscious unity with Pure Spirit; there is but One and that One is everywhere. I am one with the Eternal Consciousness."

IDEALIZATION

Form a mental picture of yourself as you want to be, and at the greatest height your imagination can picture. Dwell upon this for some time, holding the thought: "This is what I really am; it is a picture of my own soul. I am this now in soul, and I am becoming this in outward manifestation."

REALIZATION

"I appropriate to myself the power to become what I want to be, and to do what I want to do. I exercise creative energy; all the power there is mine. I will arise and go forward with power and perfect confidence; I will do excellent works in the strength of the Supreme, my God. I will trust and not fear, for Spirit is with me."

SUMMARY

TRUTHS TO THE SCIENCE OF BECOMING EXCELLENT

All people are made of the One Intelligent Substance, and therefore all contain the same essential powers and possibilities. Greatness is equally inherent in all, and may be manifested by all. Every person may become great. Every constituent of Universal Principle is a constituent of us all.

We may overcome both heredity and circumstance by exercising the inherent creative power of the soul. If you are to become great, the soul must act, and must rule the mind and the body. Your knowledge is limited, and you make mistakes through ignorance; to avoid this you must connect your soul with Universal Spirit.

Universal Spirit is the intelligent substance from which all things come; it is in and through all things. All things are known to this Universal Mind, and you can so unite yourself with it as to enter into all knowledge.

To do this: ✸ You must eliminate from yourself everything which separates you from Source. You must will to live the Divine Life, and you must rise above all moral temptations. ✸ You must abandon every course of action that is not in accord with your highest ideals.

✸ You must reach the right viewpoint, recognizing that Spirit is the All-Being, in all, and that there is nothing wrong. ✸ You must see that nature, society, government, and industry are perfect in their present stage, and advancing toward completion; and that all men and women everywhere are good and perfect. ✸ You must know that all is right with the world, and unite with Intelligence for the completion of the perfect task. It is only as you see the One as the Great Advancing Presence in all, and good in all, that you can rise to real excellence.

✱ You must consecrate yourself to the service of the highest that is within yourself, obeying the voice of the soul. There is an Inner Light in everyone which continuously impels us toward the highest, and you must be guided by this Light if you would become great.

✱ You must recognize the fact that you are one with the Father-Mother, and consciously affirm this unity for yourself and for all others. ✱ You must know yourself to be a god among gods, and act accordingly. ✱ You must have absolute faith in your own perceptions of truth, and begin at home to act upon these perceptions. As you see the true and right course in small things, you must take that course. ✱ You must cease to act unthinkingly, and begin to THINK; and you must be sincere in your thought.

✱ You must form a mental visualization of yourself at the highest, and hold this conception until it is your habitual thought-form of yourself. This thought-form you must keep continuously in view. ✱ You must outwardly realize and express the thought-form in your actions. ✱ You must do everything that you do in a great way. In dealing with your family, your neighbors, acquaintances, and friends, you must make every act an expression of your ideal.

The man or woman who reaches the right viewpoint and makes full consecration, and who fully idealizes themselves as great, and who makes every act, however trivial, an expression of the ideal, has already achieved the path to excellence. Everything they do will be done in a great way. They will make themselves known, and will be recognized as personalities of power. They will receive knowledge by inspiration, and will know all that they need to know. They will receive all the material wealth they form in their thoughts, and will not lack for any good thing. They will be given abilities to deal with any combination of circumstances which may arise, and their growth and progress will be continuous and rapid. Great works will seek them out, and everyone will delight to do them honor.

Because of its peculiar value to the reader of *The Science of Becoming Excellent*, we close this book by giving a portion of Emerson's essay on the "Oversoul." This great essay is fundamental, showing the foundation principles of monism and the science of excellence. We recommend that you study it most carefully in connection with this book.

AFTERWORD: THE OVERSOUL

by Ralph Waldo Emerson

What is the universal sense of want and ignorance, but the fine innuendo by which the great soul makes its enormous claim? Why do men feel that the natural history of man has never been written, but always he is leaving behind what you have said of him, and it becomes old, and books of metaphysics worthless? The philosophy of six thousand years has not searched the chambers and magazines of the soul. In its experiments there has always remained, in the last analysis, a residuum it could not resolve. Man is a stream whose source is hidden. Always our being is descending into us from we know not whence. The most exact calculator has no prescience that somewhat incalculable may not balk the very next moment. I am constrained every moment to acknowledge a higher origin for events than the will I call mine.

As with events, so it is with thoughts. When I watch that flowing river, which, out of regions I see not, pours for a season its streams into me –

I see that I am a pensioner – not a cause, but a surprised spectator of this ethereal water; that I desire and look up, and put myself in the attitude for reception, but from some alien energy the visions come.

The Supreme Critic on all the errors of the past and present, and the only prophet of that which must be, is that great nature in which we rest, as the earth lies in the soft arms of the atmosphere; that Unity, that Oversoul, with which every man's particular being is contained and made one with all other; that common heart, of which all sincere conversation is the worship, to which all right action is submission; that overpowering reality which confutes our tricks and talents, and constrains every one to pass for what he is, and to speak from his character and not from his tongue; and which evermore tends and aims to pass into our thought and hand, and become wisdom, and virtue, and power, and beauty. We live in succession, in division, in parts, in particles. Meantime within man is the soul of the whole; the wise silence; the universal beauty, to which every part and particle is equally related; the eternal One. And this deep power in which we exist, and whose beatitude is all accessible to us, is not only self-sufficing and perfect in every hour, but the act of seeing, and the thing seen, the seer and the spectacle, the subject and the object, are one. We see the world piece by piece, as the sun, the moon, the animal, the tree; but the whole, of which these are the shining parts, is the soul. It is only by the vision of that Wisdom, that the horoscope of the ages can be read, and it is only by falling back on our better thoughts, by yielding to the spirit of prophecy which is innate in every man, that we know what it says. Every man's words, who speaks from that life, must sound vain to those who do not dwell in the same thought on their own part. I dare not speak for it. My words do not carry its august sense; they fall short and cold. Only itself can inspire whom it will, and behold! their speech will be lyrical and sweet, and universal as the rising of the wind. Yet I desire, even by profane words, if sacred I may not use, to indicate the heaven of this deity, and to report what hints I have collected of the transcendent simplicity and energy of the Highest Law.

If we consider what happens in conversation, in reveries, in remorse, in times of passion, in surprises, in the instruction of dreams wherein often we see ourselves in masquerade — the droll disguises only magnifying and enhancing a real element, and forcing it on our distinct notice — we will catch many hints that will broaden and lighten into knowledge of the secret of nature. All goes to show that the soul in man is not an organ, but animates and exercises all the organs; is not a function, like the power of memory, of calculation, of comparison — but uses these as hands and feet; is not a faculty, but a light; is not the intellect or the will, but the master of the intellect and the will — is the vast background of our being, in which they lie — an immensity not possessed and that cannot be possessed. From within or from behind, a light shines through us upon things, and makes us aware that we are nothing, but the light is all. A man is the facade of a temple wherein all wisdom and all good abide. What we commonly call man, the eating, drinking, planting, counting man, does not, as we know him, represent himself, but misrepresents himself. Him we do not respect, but the soul, whose organ he is, would he let it appear through his action, would make our knees bend. When it breathes through his intellect, it is genius; when it flows through his affection it is love. * * * *

After its own law and not by arithmetic is the rate of its progress to be computed. The soul's advances are not made by gradation, such as can be represented by motion in a straight line; but rather by ascension of state, such as can be represented by metamorphosis – from the egg to the worm, from the worm to the fly. The growths of genius are of a certain total character, that does not advance the elect individual first over John, then Adam, then Richard, and give to each the pain of discovered inferiority, but by every throe of growth the man expands there where he works, passing, at each pulsation, classes, populations of men. With each divine impulse the mind rends the thin rinds of the visible and finite, and comes out into eternity, and inspires and expires its air. It converses with truths that have always been spoken in the world, and becomes conscious of a closer sympathy with Zeno and Arrian, than with persons in the house.

This is the law of moral and of mental gain. The simple rise as by specific levity, not into a particular virtue, but into the region of all the virtues. They are in the spirit which contains them all. The soul is superior to all the particulars of merit. The soul requires purity, but purity is not it; requires justice, but justice is not that; requires beneficence, but is somewhat better: so that there is a kind of descent and accommodation felt when we leave speaking of moral nature, to urge a virtue which it enjoins. For, to the soul in her pure action, all the virtues are natural, and not painfully acquired. Speak to his heart, and the man becomes suddenly virtuous.

Within the same sentiment is the germ of intellectual growth, which obeys the same law. Those who are capable of humility, of justice, of love, of aspiration, are already on a platform that commands the sciences and arts, speech and poetry, action and grace. For whosoever dwells in this mortal beatitude, does already anticipate those special powers which men prize so highly; just as love does justice to all the gifts of the object beloved. The lover has no talent, no skill, which passes for quite nothing with his enamored maiden, however little she may possess of related faculty. And the heart which abandons itself to the Supreme Mind finds itself related to all its works and will travel a royal road to particular knowledge and powers. For, in ascending to this primary and aboriginal sentiment, we have come from our remote station on the circumference instantaneously to the center of the world, where, as in the closet of God, we see causes, and anticipate the universe, which is but a slow effect.

WALLACE D. WATTLES

Wallace Wattles spent his entire life working out the principles and methods of the science outlined in this book. Through trial and error and much study and thought, he honed and polished his methods, and in the final years of his life, using these principles and actions, he began to manifest excellence. He truly was a genius.

Born in the late 1800's, the major portion of his life was cursed by failures. Writes his daughter Florence, "He lost a good position in the Methodist Church because of his *heresy*. He met George D. Herron at a convention of reformers in Chicago in 1896 and caught Herron's social vision. From that day, until his death, he worked unceasingly to realize the glorious vision of human brotherhood."

Florence continues, "He wrote almost constantly... in his later years (while living in Elwood, Illinois). It was then that he formed his mental picture. He saw himself as a successful writer, a personality of power, an advancing man, and he began to work toward the realization of this vision... He lived every page of his books *(The Science of Getting Rich, The Science of Becoming Excellent,* and *The Science of Well-Being).* His life was truly THE POWERFUL LIFE."

Wattles was a pioneer, and like the early trappers, he blazed the trails which became the freeways, in this case, to excellence.

DR. JUDITH POWELL

Dr. Judith Powell knows that your real treasure lies hidden within, and she has shared her secrets with thousands in the U.S.A., Europe and the Orient.

An internationally sought-after authority and speaker on expanding human excellence, Judith has written definitive articles for business and the general community on numerous enlightening topics. She has also co-authored the self-improvement book, *Silva Mind Mastery For The '90s*, distributed worldwide and translated into seventeen languages. She is currently writing *A Date With Destiny*, a book on universal truths.

Judith's popular motivational seminars include: Color Dynamics, Loving Yourself, Discover Your Perfect Mate, Dreams and Destiny, An Introduction to Neuro Linguistic Programming, and Silva Mind Mastery. She also helps others find direction to excellence through her Mind Counseling.

After receiving her Bachelor's Degree in Color Design and Business at Marygrove College in Michigan, she earned her Master's and Doctorate Degrees in Psychorientology at the Institute of Psychorientology, Texas, as well as her Masters and Trainers Certifications in Neuro Linguistic Programming (the language of the brain).

Judith, an award-winning TV host for *It's All In Your Mind*, co-directs three companies in St. Petersburg, Florida with her husband, Dr. Tag Powell. They reside in the Tampa Bay area with their three Scottish Terriers – Master, Buddha, and Isis.

THE SCIENCE OF GETTING RICH
by Wallace D. Wattles
and Dr. Judith Powell

Fantastic: a down-to-earth, clear-cut and practical approach to "How to be rich." No bones about it, when you follow the thoughts presented in this book, you will become rich, without the feeling of guilt. The authors write that the poverty-stricken (and even the middle class) should feel guilty by not living up to their true potential as Thinking Beings. It has been written about many times over, that is, "becoming rich," but when you read this rendition, you truly believe that YOU can do it! And after all, belief is the key to unlocking the door to success.

THE CLASSIC PROSPERITY BOOK

ISBN 1-56087-138-5, Trade Paperback, 160 pages

$12.95 plus $5.50 Priority Mail

THE SCIENCE OF WELL-BEING
How To Become Healthy
by Wallace D. Wattles and Dr. Judith Powell

The series continues...the message is just as powerful...and the results are even more profound! Age-old common-sense formulas for eating, breathing and sleeping your way to vibrant youthful health.

The Science of Well-Being dispels the rumors and a lifetime of misconceptions about the "right way" to healthful living. Learn the secrets for complete mental and physical health... as well as an inspirational guide to peace and well-being.

ISBN 0-914295-059-1, Trade Paperback, 160 pages

$8.95 plus $5.50 Priority Mail

Buy both books together and Save $4.00
Both Books Including Shipping...$28.90.

THINK WEALTH...

Put Your Money Where Your Mind Is!

By Dr. Tag Powell

You can become wealthy by changing your thoughts. Here, in ten easy steps, is the way to formulate and attain your money goals. A short, easy-to-read, to-the-point manual showing you how you can think wealthy and become wealthy.

* How to think rich
* How to spend rich
* How to decide your pathway to wealth
* How to plan your money moves
* How to become accustomed to wealth
* How to develop money confidence

And much, much more!

Not just another book on thinking rich -- this book is based on over two decades of research from Dr. Tag Powell's Think Wealth Seminars taught around the globe since 1979. Hundreds of thousands have claimed their increased money goals -- from $1,000 to $30 million above and beyond their normal income -- by applying these ten lessons, including:

* How to rethink your self-defeating attitudes about being wealthy.

* How to gain fresh insight into your earnings, spending, banking and investing behaviors.

Whereas "The Science of Getting Rich" covers the mental and spiritual aspects of prosperity, "Think Wealth" covers the physical and mental aspects of getting rich. With both books, you're covered: the physical, mental and spiritual truths to help YOU to greater riches.